CENTURY OF HONOR

www.ldsbsa.org

ISBN: 978-0-615-79633-8

First Printing

10 9 8 7 6 5 4 3 2 1

Printed in the United States of America

Library of Congress Control Number: 2013906832

CENTURY OF HONOR

100 YEARS OF SCOUTING IN
THE CHURCH OF JESUS CHRIST OF LATTER-DAY SAINTS

Boy Scouts of America

LDS-BSA Relationships

Norman Rockwell (1894-1978), I Will Do My Best (detail), 1943. Collection of the National Scouting Museum.

On my honor I will do my best
To do my duty to God and my country
and to obey the Scout Law;
To help other people at all times;
To keep myself physically strong,
mentally awake, and morally straight.

Boy Scout Oath or Promise, 1910–2013

"I am pleased to stand firm for an organization that teaches duty to God and country, that embraces the Scout Law. Yes, an organization whose motto is 'Be prepared' and whose slogan is 'Do a good turn daily.'"

President Thomas S. Monson

CONTENTS

Norman Rockwell (1894-1978), We Thank Thee, O' Lord *(detail), 1972. Collection of the National Scouting Museum.*

FOREWORD

LDS-BSA Centennial Patch

On May 21, 1913, The Church of Jesus Christ of Latter-day Saints officially affiliated with the Boy Scouts of America. Since the beginnings of that dynamic partnership, millions of youth and adults have registered in LDS Church-sponsored Scouting units, and leaders of the two organizations have worked together to instill *character*, *citizenship,* and *fitness* in young men.

As the first nationally chartered organization, the LDS Church established a pattern for other religious and community groups to partner with the Boy Scouts of America, thus affecting additional youth and organizations throughout the following century.

We present this book as part of the 2013 LDS-BSA Centennial Celebration. It is our sincere desire that readers will recognize the inspired decisions, leadership, and goodwill evident throughout the past "century of honor" between The Church of Jesus Christ of Latter-day Saints and the Boy Scouts of America.

David L. Beck, Young Men General President
Larry M. Gibson, First Counselor, Young Men General Presidency
Adrian Ochoa, Second Counselor, Young Men General Presidency
Mark R. Francis, LDS-BSA Relationships Director

Note: This publication uses the official Scouting style guide, which requires the words *Scout* and *Scouting* to be capitalized. However, since this capitalization was not standardized until the mid-1900s, direct quotes cited from before that time may not comply with current capitalization and punctuation guidelines. The reader may also note that the term *scouting,* as used during the early 1900s, denoted an activity rather than an official organization and is therefore not capitalized when used in that context.

MIA Scout band in front of the Church Administration Building, 1920s

RECEIVED
MAY 6 1913
IMPROVEMENT ERA

May 3rd, 1913.

Mr. L. R. Martineau,
Young Men's Mutual Improvement Assn,
20 to 22 Bishop's Bldg,
Salt Lake City, Utah.

My dear Mr. Martineau:-

It gives me great pleasure to tell you that at the last meeting of our Executive Board held yesterday, the first since your letter of March 24th reached us, it was unanimously agreed to commission Dr. John H. Taylor as recommended by the Mutual Young Men's Improvement Association and to have the affiliation of the M.I.A. Scouts with the Boy Scouts of America take place in accordance with the resolutions adopted at the meeting held March 15th.

Personally, it gives me great pleasure as executive official of the Boy Scouts of America to welcome through you all of those who will actively take up Scout work under this new plan.

On Monday I will send you 200 application blanks for commissions as Scout Master, 6 copies of our handbook and 6 copies of the proof edition of our Scout Master's Manual, together with a supply of your blanks. I will also send you a dozen copies of our bulletin, "Scouting" and will be glad to serve you and those in the Association who may give us a greater opportunity to do so.

Hereafter it will be necessary for us to bill for printed matter in accordance with the prices set forth on our order blank.

Sincerely yours,

James E. West
Chief Scout Executive.

JEW:WSK

Dictated but not read.

"DO A GOOD TURN DAILY?"

PREFACE

May 3rd, 1913.

My dear Mr. Martineau: [YMMIA General Board, Athletic Committee Chairman]—

It gives me great pleasure to tell you that at the last meeting of our Executive Board held yesterday, . . . it was unanimously agreed to . . . have the affiliation of the M.I.A. Scouts with the Boy Scouts of America take place. . . .

Personally, it gives me great pleasure as executive official of the Boy Scouts of America to welcome through you all of those who will actively take up Scout work under this new plan. . . .

Sincerely yours,
James E. West
Chief Scout Executive.

"Joseph Smith was just the age of a young Scout when he witnessed the greatest manifestation ever given to man—he was just a boy."
—Matthew O. Cowley, Quorum of the Twelve Apostles, Improvement Era, Feb. 1951, 100

CHAPTER 1

ZION'S YOUTH
1870–1910

The great movement of the Church from Illinois and Iowa to these mountains, in 1847 . . .
developed among both men and women the highest art of scoutcraft, perhaps that has been found
among any pioneers in the history of our country.

—Lyman R. Martineau, YMMIA Athletic Committee Chairman, 1912

Joseph Smith authorized the organization of the first Young People's Improvement Association in 1843. During the following years additional societies for youth were established among the Saints; however, there was no central Churchwide organization until several decades later.

On May 21, 1913, The Church of Jesus Christ of Latter-day Saints officially affiliated as a chartered organization with the Boy Scouts of America. While this date marked the beginning of an inspired partnership, the foundations of the dynamic LDS-BSA relationship were actually laid many years earlier.

The vanguard company of Mormon pioneers entered the Salt Lake Valley on July 24, 1847. Within thirty years, settlements had been established throughout Utah and the American West, a university was founded, and construction was started on three temples. The desert began to "blossom as a rose," and Zion and its people were flourishing.

Despite the prosperity of the Saints, however, a general concern was felt among Church leaders regarding the youth of Zion. By 1880, 44 percent of Utah's population was fourteen years old or younger, and according to one record, "Zion had its share of misbehavers."[1] In an effort to more fully teach and train Latter-day youth, Church auxiliary organizations were established during the 1860s and 1870s.

The YMMIA

President Brigham Young felt a special concern for the young men of the Church, observing that boys often had plenty of leisure time yet very few organized intellectual and recreational activities. In June 1875, President Brigham Young instructed recently returned missionary Elder Junius F. Wells to organize "a society of young men for mutual improvement."[2]

Junius F. Wells was the son of Church leader Daniel H. Wells and Hannah Corrilla Free. He graduated from the University of Deseret at the age of seventeen and then served a mission to Great Britain (1872-1874). Brother Wells was twenty-one years old when the YMMIA was organized.

"Let the keynote of your work be the establishment in the youth of individual testimony of the truth and . . . the development of the gifts within them, . . . cultivating a knowledge and an application of the eternal principles of the great science of life."

—President Brigham Young, as cited by B.H. Roberts, *Americana*, vol. 10 (1915), 54

Young boys playing marbles, early 1900s

During the late 1800s, deacons performed a variety of duties, including collecting fast offerings, cutting firewood for the poor, delivering food, acting as meetinghouse custodians, and passing the sacrament.

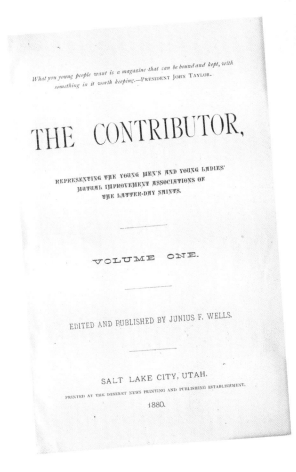

Junius Wells published the Contributor, a magazine that contained articles and lessons to support the YMMIA. The Improvement Era replaced the Contributor in 1897.

Establishment of Church Auxiliaries

Sunday School 1867	Young Ladies' Mutual Improvement Association 1869	Young Men's Mutual Improvement Association 1875	Primary Association 1878

1865   1870   1875   1880

Young boys in Sunday dress, early 1900s

Elder Wells called a meeting in the Salt Lake City Thirteenth Ward on June 10 and formally organized the first Young Men's Mutual Improvement Association (YMMIA). He later recorded, "The spirit of the work fell upon me from the moment I was chosen to undertake it."[3] The purpose of the new organization was to "help young men develop their gifts, to stand up and speak, and to bear testimony."[4] By 1890 over 11,000 young men were enrolled in the YMMIA.

Priesthood Organization Changes

The teaching of Zion's youth had gained special attention in the Church, yet it was still common for both Aaronic Priesthood and Melchizedek Priesthood offices to be filled by grown men. A First Presidency letter on July 11, 1877, reorganized and standardized priesthood quorums and offices, with an emphasis on young men serving in the Aaronic Priesthood. The letter stated, "It would be excellent training for the young men if they had the opportunity of acting in the offices of the lesser priesthood."[5] Within a year, the practice of ordaining boys to the Aaronic Priesthood was well established, and hundreds of young men became deacons.

Although new priesthood guidelines introduced young boys to quorum activity, specific duties and ages had not yet been clearly assigned. Deacons throughout the Church performed a variety of services, such as cutting firewood, delivering food to the poor, and passing the sacrament.

> "A source of strength had been opened up through the organization of the Aaronic Priesthood, the young men acquitting themselves creditably."
> —A Cache Valley bishop, 1877

> "The [YMMIA] organization spread with astonishing rapidity, and in a few months, towns where there had been crowds of uncouth boys loitering around the stores, hollowing in the streets and breaking horses on the Sabbath day, a change was seen. In some cases the roughest of these boys had been chosen for presidents of associations."
> —*Contributor*, Oct. 1879, 13

Changes in Age of Ordination 1908–1970			
	Deacon	Teacher	Priest	Elder
1908	12	15	18	21
1925	12	15	17	20
1934	12	15	17	19
1953	12	15	17	20
1954	12	14	16	20
1960	12	14	16	19
1970	12	14	16	18

*In 1910, Bryant S. Hinckley,
a member of the YMMIA general board
and father of future Church President
Gordon B. Hinckley, traveled to
Chicago, New York, Boston,
and other cities to study gymnasiums
and athletics. He returned to Utah and
assisted in establishing the Deseret
Gymnasium in Salt Lake City,
serving as general secretary and
manager. Brother Hinckley felt
that the new facility would help
Latter-day youth live
"nobler and better lives."[10]*

Recreation and Religion

Around the turn of the twentieth century, leaders throughout the United States became increasingly concerned about the attitude of leisure spreading among American youth. Boys were not always required to plow fields, tend to animals, and perform rigorous physical labor. Historian Edward Rowan wrote, "There was a general feeling in the early years of the twentieth century that immigration, movement into the cities, and the loss of the frontier had weakened the youth of America."[6]

In Utah, Church members shared similar concerns about the moral and mental well-being of their young people. Many parents and grandparents of the generation had pulled handcarts or driven wagons across the plains, yet their children and grandchildren were growing up in a society of increased ease and opportunity. Church leaders felt a pressing need to adopt new teaching methods and activity programs that would strengthen and appeal to youth.

During the April 1903 general conference, President Joseph F. Smith encouraged manual training for young men so that "the nobility of practical labor, and the contentment arising therefrom, will be more clearly manifest among the people."[7] Five years later, in the opening address of the April 1908 general conference, he requested that boys be given "something to do that will make them interested in the work of the Lord."[8]

In response to President Smith's 1908 request, reforms known as the "Priesthood Movement" were proposed. It was recommended that each boy move systematically through Aaronic Priesthood offices with fixed ages. These ages established the basis for priesthood quorums and classes.

The YMMIA general board also passed a resolution to "take up educational, literary, and recreative studies, permeated by religious thought" and resolved that "athletic work be encouraged and established wherever practicable."[9]

Despite some hesitation from older Church members about combining recreation and religion, the introduction of athletic activities to the YMMIA resulted in an astounding response from the young men. Youth attendance increased significantly, and missionary work was performed naturally as the young men brought their friends to YMMIA meetings and activities. The standardization of priesthood ages and additional emphasis on recreation laid the foundation for a new era of training young men within the Church.

"Athletic work had the effect of drawing nearly all
of the junior boys in the ward to the meetings. . . .
The officers of the M.I.A. . . . have not found it necessary
to do any missionary work. . . . The boys themselves have
done it by bringing their companions to Mutual."

—*Improvement Era*, Aug. 1909, 840-841

The Deseret Gym opened on September 20, 1910, and was "the largest and best equipped institution in the intermountain district." —Improvement Era, *Feb. 1910, 381*

First Scout Camp at Brownsea Island, Summer 1907

CHAPTER 2

THE SCOUTING MOVEMENT 1907–1910

Our aim in the [Scouting] Movement is to give such help as we can in bringing about God's Kingdom on earth, by inculcating among youth the spirit and the daily practice in their lives of unselfish goodwill and co-operation.

—Lord Robert Baden-Powell

Lord Baden-Powell gained fame throughout the British Empire during the Second Boer War. He became known as the "Hero of Mafeking" after his intelligent strategies led his soldiers and the local townspeople of Mafeking, South Africa, through a 216-day siege, October 13, 1899–May 17, 1900.

Concern for the moral upbringing of young people was not only felt by Church leaders, but also by youth leaders around the world.

The Boy Scout movement was founded in 1907 by Englishman Lord Robert Stephenson Smyth Baden-Powell. Born February 22, 1857, in London, England, "Stephe" was the son of Reverend Baden Powell, an Oxford professor, and Henrietta Grace Smyth. He enjoyed a happy family life and often spent time outdoors with his brothers—boating, hiking, and tracking. After graduating from Charterhouse, a prestigious public school, he joined the British military in 1876 and traveled to India as a lieutenant. Baden-Powell served for the next thirty years in various military assignments in India and South Africa. In 1897, he became a colonel, and in May

of 1900, at the age of forty-three, was promoted to major general, the youngest in the British army. He returned to England in 1903, and retired in 1910 as a lieutenant general.

Aids to Scouting

During his military tours, Baden-Powell wrote a book, *Aids to Scouting,* designed to teach soldiers basic scouting and outdoor skills. After returning to England, Baden-Powell discovered that *Aids to Scouting* was not only read by soldiers but was also popular among young boys, teachers, and youth organizations. He revised his book to specifically train boys—rather than soldiers—in scouting skills, and envisioned a new program that would teach youth about outdoor life while simultaneously building character.

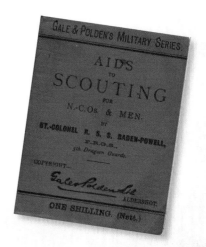

Chief Scout of the World,
Lord Robert Baden-Powell

Scouting for Boys was published in six installments in 1908, and sold approximately 150 million copies as the fourth best-selling book of the 20th century.

During his lifetime, Baden-Powell saw his Scouting movement encompass over thirty-two countries with more than 3.3 million Scouts. In his farewell message he stated, "I believe that God put us in this jolly world to be happy and enjoy life. Happiness does not come from being rich, nor merely being successful in your career. . . . The real way to get happiness is by giving out happiness to other people. Try and leave this world a little better than you found it."

Norman Rockwell (1894-1978). A Daily Good Turn (detail), 1918. Collection of the National Scouting Museum.

In August 1907, Baden-Powell organized an experimental "scouting" encampment at Brownsea Island. Twenty boys were organized into four patrols and spent several days camping, working, hiking, and learning about nature. Principles such as honesty, cheerfulness, and service were integrated throughout the activities. Upon completion of the camp, Baden-Powell concluded that boys could learn valuable life lessons through participation in outdoor adventures. These ideas were incorporated into his revised book, *Scouting for Boys*, which was published in 1908.

Although he professed no intentions of starting an organization, Baden-Powell's Scouting movement spread rapidly around the globe. Boys everywhere rallied around the promise of adventure through outdoor activities. The enthusiasm of both youth and adults carried the movement forward at an astonishing pace, and Scout troops were soon organized throughout the world.

The Boy Scouts of America

The transport of the Boy Scout movement across the Atlantic Ocean is credited to American publisher William D. Boyce. While en route to an African safari in 1909, he became lost while traveling through London, England. A young English boy—later known as the "Unknown Scout"—offered to help and led Mr. Boyce to his destination. Grateful for the boy's service, Mr. Boyce tried to pay him. The helpful lad refused the tip, stating that he was a Boy Scout and didn't take money for performing a good turn.

Mr. Boyce was impressed with the young man and inquired further about the Boy Scout movement. He later visited the Scouting headquarters in London and returned to America with information about the growing program. The Boy Scouts of America was incorporated in the District of Columbia on February 8, 1910. Incorporation allowed the Boy Scouts of America to copyright their logo, program, and resources and helped streamline various Scouting groups into one organization.

William Boyce turned the leadership of his new program over to Edgar M. Robinson (international YMCA secretary), who assembled Daniel Carter Beard (founder of the Sons of Daniel Boone), Ernest Thompson Seton (founder of the Woodcraft Indians), and other American youth leaders to assist in organizing the Boy Scouts of America. By November 1910, a volunteer National Council of thirty-five leading citizens had been formed, with U.S. President Howard W. Taft accepting the Honorary Presidency. James E. West, a young lawyer in Washington, D.C., was invited to be the executive secretary of the new organization. On January 2, 1911, Mr. West opened the headquarters in rented offices in New York City with seven employees. The following November he became the first Chief Scout Executive.

Publisher William D. Boyce employed up to 30,000 newsboys. He felt that Scouting would teach them valuable skills and self-sufficiency.

"How many boys have had their lives blessed—even saved—by the Scout movement begun by Baden-Powell? . . . Baden-Powell had neither sailed the stormy seas of glory nor founded empires of worldly wealth. Rather, he was a builder of boys, one who taught them well how to run and win the race of life."
—President Thomas S. Monson, *Church News*, May 19, 2007, 3

James E. West was orphaned at age six. As a young teenager, he directed recreation and education for boys at the orphanage where he lived. He was a practicing attorney in Washington, D. C., active in the YMCA, and a motivating force in the first White House Conference on Youth.
Mr. West agreed to assist the new Scouting organization for a period of six months, during which time he commuted between his law practice in Washington, D.C., and the New York City Boy Scout headquarters.
He eventually devoted his time entirely to Scouting and served for thirty-two years as the executive officer of the Boy Scouts of America.

Scouting founders: Ernest Thompson Seton, Robert Stephenson Smyth Baden-Powell, and Daniel Carter Beard

"I feel grateful to the Lord that Sir Robert Baden-Powell was impressed—may I say, inspired—to give scouting to the world."

—President George Albert Smith, *Improvement Era*, Sep. 1948, 558

"Every boy has in him a little savage and a potential good citizen. The question is which is to get the upper grip; upon that depends what kind of a man he is going to be. . . . Scouting [will not] make an angel of him at once . . . [but] it gives him the right start."
—Jacob A. Riis, social reformer, 1910 BSA National Council Board member, *Improvement Era*, July 1914, 869

Early National Council Board members included American author Henry Van Dyke, Colonel Theodore Roosevelt, social reformer Jacob A. Riis, former Secretary of the Interior James R. Garfield, and other prominent men of the day. President Howard W. Taft accepted the Honorary Presidency.

By 1911 national BSA membership had reached

61,495

1911 Boy Scout health standards were in harmony with the Word of Wisdom:

"The average boy ought to have and usually does have an appetite like an ostrich.

"Don't eat too much . . . don't eat meat more than once a day. . . .

"Drink freely of clean water between meals.

"Growing boys especially should have nothing to do with tea, coffee, or any stimulant.

"Alcohol is not a stimulant, but is really a narcotic that is very depressing. . . . The same is true of nicotine in tobacco. "No growing boy should use either."

—*Handbook for Boys,* 1911

Scouting Comes to Utah

Scouting spread rapidly across America. Boys everywhere wanted to experience the adventure and fun of the new outdoor program.

Thomas George Wood, an English Latter-day Saint emigrant in Salt Lake City, Utah, learned about the Boy Scout movement from his uncle in England. In September 1910, after taking a hike and doing "lots of thinking," he resolved to "do all in my power to start the Boy Scout Movement in the ward for the good of our boys." After some additional research, Brother Wood shared his plans with the boys of the Salt Lake City Waterloo Ward, and received "lots of enthusiasm and encouragement."[11] He proposed the organization of a ward Scout troop to his bishop, Asael H. Woodruff, son of Church President Wilford Woodruff, who agreed to the idea.

The ward had more than fifty boys over the age of twelve, who were "noisy and not easy to manage."[12] Using the guidance of an English Scout manual, Brother Wood organized a troop on October 12, 1910. The first Scout meeting was held a week later.

Other wards soon organized Scout troops within their YMMIA organizations. Even though the Church was not officially affiliated with the Boy Scouts of America, some ward troops operated under the direction of the National Boy Scout Council. The inspired Scouting movement of Englishman Baden-Powell had reached across seas and plains to the youth of Zion.

The first Scout meeting of the Waterloo Ward Scout Troop consisted of a flag ceremony, close-order drills, calisthenics, and games. Brother Wood was "much pleased in the spirit shown."
—Thomas George Wood Diary, vol. 13, Oct. 19, 1910

Thomas George Wood was twenty-three years old when he received his commission as Scoutmaster.

"Even now, 40 years and two world wars later, I remain at heart a Boy Scout, full of admiration for the qualities I have seen develop in boys and young men because of scouting."

—Thomas George Wood writings, 21

During their first campout, Brother Wood and fifteen boys
rode a streetcar to Holladay in southeast Salt Lake County.
They then hiked fourteen miles up Big Cottonwood Canyon,
with their supplies piled on a horse-drawn wagon. The troop
camped at the Brighton recreational area. "Discipline was
strict," he recorded. "If any of the boys got out of line they
had to take up their own blankets and carry them."
Brother Wood served as Scoutmaster for fifteen years.
—Deseret News, Jan. 6, 1964

World Scout Fleur-de-lis

The fleur-de-lis is the basic shape of badges used by Scout organizations around the world. It is a modified form of the sign of the north on the mariner's compass and is meant to remind the Scout to point the right way in life.

Several historical documents record that the first LDS Scout troop was the First Aetna Troop, formed in the Aetna Ward, Cardston, Canada. Bishop Nathan W. Tanner called James Henry Tanner to serve as Scoutmaster. Bishop Tanner's son, N. Eldon Tanner (back row, third from right), would later serve in the Church's First Presidency. In 1914 the Boy Scouts of Canada was officially organized and received a national charter.

"The only equipment [the Boy Scout Movement] needs is the outdoors, a group of boys, and a leader."

—1911 Handbook for Boys *as cited in* Improvement Era, *Apr. 1911*

CHAPTER 3

MIA SCOUTS
1911–1913

If the Boy Scout Organization can take the New York City lad out into the forests of New York State and . . . develop in him a wholesome sympathy for and appreciation of the work done by the early pathfinders of America, how much more so could such a movement here in the west among the "Mormons" bring the youth of Zion into close and lasting relationship with our fathers and forefathers.

—Eugene L. Roberts, Director of Physical Training, Brigham Young University

President Joseph F. Smith was the prophet when Scouting was organized in the Church.

Scouting continued to grow in Utah. On March 8, 1911, the Church's YMMIA board organized a committee to study the movement and investigate the possibility of standardizing Boy Scout troops within the YMMIA by affiliating with the national organization. Committee members included Brigham H. Roberts (YMMIA 2nd counselor), George H. Brimhall (president of BYU), and Benjamin Goddard (YMMIA general board member). On Wednesday, March 22, 1911, they presented their report to the YMMIA general superintendent and general board.

"The spirit of the [Scouting] organization seems to be character-building by acquiring ability to do common things. . . . It encourages out-door life and has a dash in it of patriotism."[13]

After giving a full report on the origin, organization, and purposes of the Boy Scouts, the committee concluded with the following, "Your committee, while recognizing the very great excellence of the Boy Scout Movement in and of itself, feel no necessity . . . for entering into confederation with such separate units and other organizations taking up scout work."

The committee further recommended, "We have not given sufficient attention to out-door life and activities for our junior members" and suggested that "the 'Athletics and Field-sports'

> "Of the general excellence and practicability and desirability of the Boy Scout Movement . . . there can be no doubt."
> —*Report on Scouting to the YMMIA*, Mar. 22, 1911

Boys' Life *magazine was founded and published by George S. Barton of Somerville, Massachusetts. The March 1911 edition featured 48 pages and a two-color cover. The purpose of the publication was to give Scouts a magazine "they could call their own," and "which they will not be afraid to have their parents see them reading."*

"The pale, city-bred boy, who has never camped on the deseret [sic], nor seen the wilds, who has never tramped over the hills, nor 'roughed' it, cannot truly sympathize with the struggles of his father."
—Eugene L. Roberts, Director of Physical Training at Brigham Young University, Improvement Era, *Oct. 1911*

have its duties enlarged so as to include out-door activities that . . . will have for their purpose the promotion of ability in boys to do things that are useful to themselves and to others."[14] The YMMIA general board unanimously adopted the report as presented.

Even though the committee did not recommend official affiliation with the Boy Scouts of America, they did recognize the value of a Scouting program, and action was taken to incorporate Scouting methods within the YMMIA. Several organizations across America were using Scouting concepts— teaching outdoor skills as a tool to instill values. It seemed logical that the Church could also create its own program, completely operated by priesthood leaders, with no concern of forfeiting leadership control or religious training to a public organization.

MIA Scouts

Scouting was integrated as an official activity of the YMMIA in 1911, and an organization was formed to promote outdoor activity and skills. The *Deseret News* reported on September 2, 1911, that the purpose of Scouting within the Church was "to promote discipline and develop character, to instill honor and trustworthiness in the lives of young boys and to inspire them with a sense of duty to parents, country, and religious ideals." This Church movement replaced official Boy Scout troops already established in many wards, and "all wards and stakes were urged to take up this new work."[15]

John H. Taylor, YMMIA Athletic Director, was given the responsibility to promote MIA Scout work in the stakes and wards. He was eventually commissioned in 1913 by the Boy Scouts of America to oversee Scouting in all Church units in the western United States.

"The Boy Scout movement, which was commenced some years ago in England, met at once with such a general approval that it is scattering all over the civilized countries. It is now being taken up under the auspices of the M.I.A. and will be made an auxiliary of this prominent organization of the Church."

—*Deseret News,* Nov. 14, 1911

The purposes and plans of the MIA Scout movement were printed in the March 1912 Improvement Era. *Scout meetings were held for thirty minutes immediately before or after regular MIA meetings on Tuesday nights.*

"The boy scout of today must be chivalrous, manly, and gentlemanly. When he gets up in the morning he may tie a knot in his necktie, and leave the necktie outside his vest until he has done a good turn. . . . The scout also ought to know how to save life. . . . He must be systematically taking exercise, playing games, running, and walking. . . . The scout should be a lover of his country. He should know his country. In short, to be a good scout is to be a well-developed, well-informed boy.

"Another scout virtue is cheerfulness. As the scout law intimates, he must never go about with a sulky air. He must always be bright and smiling, and, as the humorist says, 'Must always see the doughnut and not the hole.'

"Wherever there have been heroes there have been scouts; and to be a scout means to be prepared to do the right thing at the right moment, no matter what the consequences may be.

"The final and chief test of the scout is the doing of a good turn to somebody every day, quietly and without boasting. This is the proof of the scout."

—1911 *Handbook for Boys*, as cited in *Improvement Era*, Mar. 1912, 358

Mutual Work

Saved the Child's Life

The practical nature of the M. I. A. Scout movement was well demonstrated, last month, by one of its members. While returning home from Religion Class in the Waterloo Ward, Salt Lake City, May 1, little Tessie Dalebout, age 6, slipped into Parley's Creek, a swift and turbulent stream at this season of the year. The current carried her down the stream for nearly a block, under two bridges, and tumbled her over and over. Two men saw her fall and, rushing across the fields, managed to pull her from the water, but when taken out, the little girl was full of water and apparently dead. Louis Rosenlund, 15 years of age, and patrol leader of the Waterloo troop, which is the first scout organization of the Church, beheld the men running across the field and followed them. They were working her arms and limbs, but without effect.

LOUIS ROSENLUND

TESSIE DALEBOUT

He immediately sent another scout for a doctor, and proceeded himself to use the Schaefer method, which he had been taught in the scout meetings, for the resuscitation of the drowned. After continuing this for about fifteen minutes, the child began to breathe and was taken home before the doctor arrived. She has since fully recovered. Great credit is due the lad for his presence of mind, and his quick application of the practical things learned through his scout organization, which saved the little girl's life.

Summer Work

Supt. Aaron W. Tracy of the North Weber stake and his board have prepared a summer course for the wards in their stake that

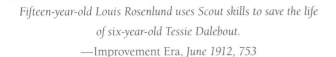

Fifteen-year-old Louis Rosenlund uses Scout skills to save the life
of six-year-old Tessie Dalebout.
—Improvement Era, *June 1912, 753*

"The great underlying purpose in incorporating scoutcraft in the M.I.A. junior activities
is the making in our boys a more rugged manhood and more self-reliant characters.
We give to the organizers of the 'Boy Scouts of America' unstinted praise for the splendid
ideas and movement they have inaugurated."
—Lyman R. Martineau, Improvement Era, *Mar. 1912, 361*

Possible names for the new Scouting organization were suggested, including the "Boy Pioneers of Utah," the "MIA Craftsmen," and the "MIA Rangers." The name "MIA Scouts" was officially adopted on November 29, 1911. Membership included boys from twelve to eighteen years old. Soon several thousand boys were enrolled in the MIA Scouts.

MIA Scout troops were organized throughout Utah and other areas of the Church. From 1911 to 1913, the Church Scouting movement grew in both membership and enthusiasm. The benefits of teaching and training Latter-day Saint youth through outdoor skills and activities were established. The organization of the MIA Scouts had laid the foundation for a national partnership to be formed.

MIA Scouts in action

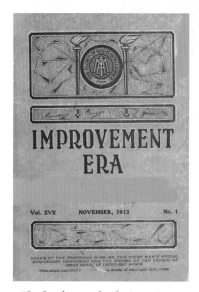

The first lessons for the MIA Scouts were published in the Improvement Era. Subjects included woodcraft, organization, leadership, knot tying, bandaging, first aid, troop discipline and efficiency, the history of the flag, physical development, astronomy, orienteering, and other outdoor skills.

From July 21, 1912, to July 24, 1912, MIA Scouts marched and camped "over the pioneer trail" from Echo Canyon, Utah, through Henefer, East Canyon, Mountain Dell, and over Little Mountain to Liberty Park in Salt Lake City. At Liberty Park, they formed into columns and marched in the Pioneer Day parade. The purpose of the event was to "obtain inspiration for the admirable work of the pioneers, to enjoy a pleasant outing, and to get some education in nature, discipline, and history." —Improvement Era, Sep. 1912, 1038

"When we established Scouting in America, we took the English Scout Laws and adapted them to our needs. Then we added the tenth law—'A Scout is Brave,' and the eleventh law—'A Scout is Clean,' and the twelfth law—'A Scout is Reverent.'"

—James E. West,
National Convention Speech,
July 4, 1937, 21

The Scout Law
Scouting for Boys, 1908

A Scout's honour is to be trusted.

A Scout is loyal to the King, and to his officers, and to his country, and to his employers.

A Scout's duty is to be useful and to help others.

A Scout is a friend to all, and a brother to every other Scout, no matter to what social class the other belongs.

A Scout is courteous.

A Scout is a friend to animals.

A Scout obeys orders of his patrol leader or scout master without question.

A Scout smiles and whistles under all circumstances.

A Scout is thrifty.

The Scout Law
Boy Scouts of America, "Seton Handbook," 1910

A Scout's honor is to be trusted.

A Scout is loyal to his country, his officers, his parents and his employers.

A Scout's duty is to be useful and to help others.

A Scout is a friend to all, and a brother to every other scout, no matter to what social class the other belongs.

A Scout is courteous.

A Scout is a friend to animals.

A Scout obeys orders of his parents, patrol leader, or scoutmaster without question.

A Scout smiles and looks pleasant under all circumstances.

A Scout is thrifty.

The Scout Law
Handbook for Boys, 1911

A Scout is trustworthy.

A Scout is loyal.

A Scout is helpful.

A Scout is friendly.

A Scout is courteous.

A Scout is kind.

A Scout is obedient.

A Scout is cheerful.

A Scout is thrifty.

A Scout is brave.

A Scout is clean.

A Scout is reverent.

MIA Scout Ideals
Improvement Era, 1912

A Scout must:

Be clean.

Stand erect.

Keep his self-respect.

Be manly.

Be courageous.

Be cheerful.

Be industrious.

Maintain individuality.

Believe in God and right living.

"In training our Scouts . . . don't let the technical outweigh the moral. Field efficiency, back woodsmanship, camping, hiking, Good Turns, jamboree comradeship are all means, not the end. The end is CHARACTER with a purpose."

—Lord Robert Baden-Powell

A flag ceremony at an early LDS Boy Scout campout

CHAPTER 4

THE EARLY YEARS
1913–1919

There is no religious side to the movement. The whole of it is based on religion,

that is, on the realisation and service of God.

—Lord Robert Baden-Powell

The Boy Scouts of America gained momentum and popularity across the country. By January 1913, over 6,000 troops and 300,000 boys were active in the growing movement. The MIA Scouts organization continued to grow as well, and by January 1913, approximately 1,500 troops and 20,000 boys were involved in the Church program.

John H. Taylor, YMMIA athletic director, traveled among Church stakes promoting and assisting with MIA Scouting. He was often asked why the MIA Scouts were not affiliated with the national organization of the Boy Scouts of America. The question was posed to the YMMIA Athletic Committee, and it was suggested that Brother Taylor informally investigate the advantages and disadvantages of affiliation in order to make a recommendation to the general board. After reviewing available Boy Scout literature and interviewing several gentlemen, he contacted the national organization for assistance. National Field Scout Commissioner Samuel A. Moffat was en route to the West Coast on Scouting business, and a meeting was arranged in Salt Lake City.

On the morning of Wednesday, January 8, 1913, Commissioner Moffat met with Heber J. Grant, Brigham H. Roberts, Lyman R. Martineau, Bryant S. Hinckley, Brigham F. Grant, Oscar A. Kirkham, and John H. Taylor at the YMCA building. The mechanics of a possible partnership were discussed. The brethren wanted to know if the word "promise" could be interchanged with "oath" in the Boy Scout Oath. They also discussed the commission of a Church leader to manage Scout work in LDS troops. Commissioner Moffat emphasized maintaining national advancement standards. The Boy Scouts of America had not yet officially affiliated with any organization, and the provision for such an arrangement required forethought and discussion from both parties. Commissioner Moffat assured the Brethren that a potential affiliation would be "effective and agreeable."[16]

Lyman Royal Martineau was born April 21, 1859, in Parowan, Utah. He graduated from Brigham Young College in Logan, Utah, in 1879 and was preparing to study law at Cornell University in New York when he was called on a mission to Great Britain. He served on the YMMIA general board from 1905 to 1926 and was described as having a "pleasing personality, sympathetic, and kindly in disposition."

—Deseret News, Jan. 6, 1926

Samuel A. Moffat was hired in 1910 as a financial secretary for the Boy Scouts of America and was promoted to Field Scout Commissioner in 1911. He traveled around the country meeting with Scout groups.

The YMMIA Athletic Committee recommended affiliation with the Boy Scouts of America for five reasons:

Broader opportunities as Scouts

Definiteness of purpose and standardization of merit

A general uplift and fellowship of the boys of the nation

The missionary work of our boys, associating with their fellows

A worthy spirit of fellowship and brotherhood with the national organization

At the general board meeting that evening, Athletic Committee Chairman Lyman R. Martineau reported on the earlier affiliation discussion, and Heber J. Grant expressed that he had been "very favorably impressed"[17] with Mr. Moffat. It was also shared that twenty-one LDS boys in Logan, Utah, had joined the Scout troop of the Reverend Mr. Jones in order to receive the official BSA badges, reflecting the fact that some LDS young men and leaders were involved in the national Scouting program in addition to the MIA Scout activities. A motion of the board authorized the committee to further investigate a potential affiliation.

During the following weeks, Church and Scouting leaders corresponded. James E. West, Chief Scout Executive, sent copies of the BSA articles of incorporation and by-laws as well as excerpts from the BSA *Handbook for Boys* for review by YMMIA leaders.

"Trusting that this action will result in greater opportunities for good to our organizations."

Letter from YMMIA general secretary Moroni Snow to Chief Scout Executive James E. West, May 9, 1913

After several weeks of study, the Athletic Committee wrote a letter to the YMMIA general board stating, "We regard the advantages as far greater than the disadvantages of affiliation. . . . In view of all we can learn, therefore, your committee recommend affiliation with the 'Boy Scouts of America.'"[18] On February 26, 1913, the general board voted unanimously to affiliate, and requested that Athletic Director John H. Taylor be commissioned by the BSA National Council and given jurisdiction over the LDS Scouts in the western states. The following week, an official resolution to affiliate was presented to the YMMIA, and on March 15, 1913, the resolution was passed by the general board.

"Western Scout Shoes" ZCMI ad from Mar. 1913 Improvement Era

Bryant S. Hinckley presented the resolution in favor of affiliation to the general board. Elder Anthony W. Ivins carried the motion to the Twelve Apostles and First Presidency, and President Joseph F. Smith agreed to adopt the national Boy Scout program in the YMMIA.

"No scout can ever hope to amount to much until he has learned a reverence for religion."

—Boy Scouts of America, *Handbook for Boys*, 1911

A YMMIA conference was traditionally held each June, near Brigham Young's birthday (June 1) to commemorate the organization of the YMMIA by Brigham Young. June was also the beginning of the MIA year and was a time for celebration, calendaring, and starting a new curriculum.

Official Charter

Lyman R. Martineau sent a letter to James E. West on March 24, informing him that the resolution to affiliate had been adopted by the general board. On May 2, the BSA National Executive Board voted unanimously to accept the affiliation of the MIA Scouts with the Boy Scouts of America. An official charter was issued on May 21, 1913, authorizing the Church to use the Boy Scouts of America program for its boys throughout the United States as well as in Church Scout troops in Canada and Mexico.

On June 9, 1913, in conjunction with the annual MIA conference, the charter was signed and a celebration was held in honor of the affiliation between the Church and the Boy Scouts of America. Scouts gathered at Wandamere Park in Salt Lake City for a day of Scouting activities. A dynamic partnership, destined to affect millions of boys, had been formed.

"The General Board has decided to give the Saturday afternoon of the June Conference . . . to demonstrations and contest work in Boy Scout activities. The scout program will consist of life-saving, carrying and bandaging, signal work and tent raising. . . . The stakes are invited to send one or more patrols to contest in any part of the work."
—*Improvement Era*, May 1913, 741

7025. Wandamere Resort,
Salt Lake City, Utah.

Wandamere Park was a large amusement park located in South Salt Lake. Originally named Calder Park, the name was changed to Wandamere in 1909 and was located on what is today Nibley Golf Course at 2780 South 700 East, South Salt Lake, Utah.

LDS-BSA NATIONAL AFFILIATION TIMELINE

January 7-8, 1913

National Field Commissioner Samuel A. Moffat meets with YMMIA Athletic Committee members to discuss a possible partnership between the two organizations.

January 8, 1913

At a YMMIA board meeting, it is decided to further investigate official affiliation.

January 29–February 8, 1913

Chief Scout Executive James E. West sends copies of Scouting documents to Salt Lake City for review by the Athletic Committee. "We are delighted to know that there is some chance of . . . our program being made available to the boys."[19]

February 19, 1913

Lyman R. Martineau, John H. Taylor, and Oscar A. Kirkham submit a letter to the YMMIA general board recommending affiliation with the Boy Scouts of America.

February 26, 1913

After lengthy discussion, the board votes unanimously to affiliate, upon condition that John H. Taylor be commissioned by the National Council as Church Scout Commissioner.

"We sincerely believe that our leaders, who . . . brought Scouting into the Church and made it a part of the MIA program for boys, did realize that with the blessings of our Heavenly Father it would grow and develop into the wonderful program which we have today."

—Oscar A. Kirkham, 1913 YMMIA board member, *Say the Good Word*, 96

March 5, 1913	March 15, 1913	May 2, 1913	May 21, 1913	June 9, 1913
An official resolution to affiliate with the National Boy Scouts is presented by Bryant S. Hinckley on behalf of the Athletic Committee.	The resolution is passed by the YMMIA general board. Later, it is presented to the Quorum of the Twelve Apostles and President Joseph F. Smith.	The National Council Boy Scouts of America Executive Board votes to unanimously accept the MIA Scouts as the first chartered organization.	A national charter is issued; this is the official date of affiliation between The Church of Jesus Christ of Latter-day Saints and the Boy Scouts of America.	The national charter is signed at a celebration in conjunction with the June MIA conference.

The majority of early Scoutmasters had a college education, were on average 32 ½ years old, were married with sons of their own, and gave approximately 5 ½ hours of Scouting service each week.

Members of the 1913 Athletic Committee included Lyman R. Martineau as chairman, Hyrum M. Smith, and (pictured left to right) Oscar A. Kirkham, Brigham F. Grant, Bryant S. Hinckley, and John H. Taylor.

1913 Scout Uniform

The official affiliation of the MIA Scouts and the Boy Scouts of America combined the efforts and resources of two influential youth organizations. LDS young men, who had the foundations of the restored gospel of Jesus Christ, were introduced to the meaningful activities and recognitions provided by the BSA, while the nationally exploding Scouting organization gained the enthusiasm of dedicated Church leaders and youth. The synergistic partnership propelled Scouting forward across the United States and throughout the Church as Scout troops were registered in every ward.

The National Boy Scout organization noted in their 1914 annual report that "leaders of the . . . Mutual Improvement Association . . . have been doing with much enthusiasm, and at present time there are troops connected with Mormon institutions, obligated to the Scout Oath and Law and carrying out the Scout program in the same manner as all other troops of Scouts."[20]

Further commitment to the national organization occurred in December 1913, when the Church announced that twelve-year-old boys, who had formerly been members of the Primary Association, would automatically be enrolled in the YMMIA, along with young men up through age eighteen. This change harmonized the ages of Scouting and Aaronic Priesthood boys.

**Good Turns reported in "The Boy Scouts,"
by Jacob A. Riis, and printed in the
Improvement Era, July 1914**

"I get a man's paper for him every morning.

"I filled my mother's wood-box
for it was baking day.

"I buttoned Mary's dress because mama
was busy.

"I shut up the hens, so my father would
not have to.

"I done up a finger for a friend.

"My grandmother lost her glasses
and I found them.

"I separated some roosters from the pullets.

"There was a cat in a steel trap and
I went and let him out.

"I done an errand for an old lady.

"I saw a dog that was hungry and fed him."

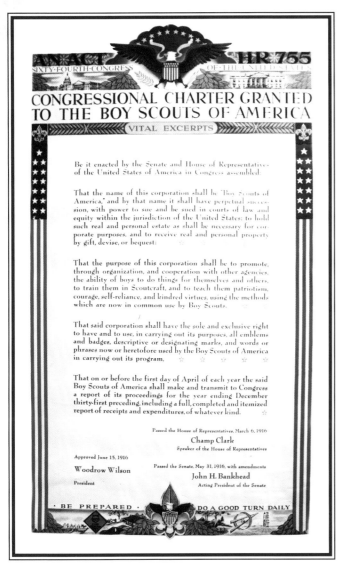

BSA Congressional Charter

Congressional Charter Granted

The Church of Jesus Christ of Latter-day Saints was the first organization to form an official affiliation with the Boy Scouts of America. This partnership not only blessed the two respective organizations but also provided a pattern for other organizations to charter Scouting units. In addition, the added strength and membership of the MIA Scouts assisted the BSA in acquiring a national charter from the Congress of the United States of America on June 15, 1916.

The Boy Scouts of America was granted a federal charter from the U.S. Congress in 1916, which gave special protection to the Boy Scout name and insignia, and limited members to U.S. citizens. The bill passed both houses unanimously and was signed by President Woodrow Wilson on June 15, 1916.

"If you find that what we offer will help you in your Youth Program, take it and use it. Build upon the temporal as a foundation for your spiritual structure. Scouting. . . leaves religion to those chosen and qualified to teach it, but declares the necessity of religion in character development and urges its practice."
—James E. West, Chief Scout Executive, National Convocation Speech, July 4, 1937, 26

In 1918, future Church President Ezra Taft Benson was commissioned as assistant Scoutmaster, and later as Scoutmaster, of his Whitney, Idaho ward Scout troop.

The General M. I. A. Conference

THE SCOUT ACTIVITIES, JUNE 8

On Thursday, 8th, there were three meetings of the Boy Scouts, the first being held in the Bishop's Building at 10 o'clock a. m. Music by the congregation, "America." Prayer by Nephi Anderson. Music by congregation, "O Ye Mountains High," Elder Heber J. Grant presided, and Elder Lyman R. Martineau conducted the exercises.

There were representatives from fifty-four stakes, including many scout masters and others interested in M. I. A. Scout work.

Charles H. Spencer, Jr., occupied fifteen minutes with a dissertation on "The Tenderfoot Scout."

John H. Taylor discussed the "Second Class Scout", including the standard of efficiency and what to do with the new boy just enrolling.

T. George Wood spoke on "The First Class Scout," standards of efficiency and scout requirements, and how to teach them.

Willard Ashton spoke on "Additional Programs," including games, socials, and the place of drill exercises.

The closing speech was made by Bryant S. Hinckley on "The Daily Good Turn," how to promote it among boys and officers. Each exercise was followed by lively discussion. The exercises closed with singing, "Count Your Blessings," and prayer by President William H. Smart, of Duchesne stake.

At 2 o'clock in the afternoon the Bishop's Building was again crowded with officers and M. I. A. Scout workers. The congregation sang, "Redeemer of Israel," and prayer was offered by Joseph G. Wood. Singing, "Sowing."

J. Karl Woods spoke on "Hikes," day and over-night, preparation, and equipment, the excellent speech will appear in full in the next number of the ERA.

National Committeeman A. W. Ivins spoke on "Summer Camps," permanent, and one season camps, preparation for them and the supervision of daily programs, their cost and the co-operation of parents.

Claude Cornwall occupied a short time giving demonstrations of scout songs, yells and signals, taking the congregation as his scout class.

CHURCH MERIT CERTIFICATE, OR BADGE

Oscar A. Kirkham followed, explaining the Church Merit badge, the relation of the scout troop to the Y. M. M. I. A., initiation ceremony, time of meeting, and the correlation of class and scout work.

Open to all Y. M. M. I. A. Boys from 12 to 20 years inclusive, including M. I. A. Boy Scouts.

After having passed the following requirements the boy is entitled to the Church Merit Badge, or Certificate, or both:

1. A complete reading of the Book of Mormon.
2. A complete reading of the New Testament.
3. Attend 75% or more of the regular Y. M. M. I. A. meetings.
4. Attend 75% or more of the regular Priesthood quorum meetings.

5. Abstain from the use of tobacco in any form.
6. Abstain from the use of liquor in any form.

The above must be accomplished and adhered to during one year from the time of application.

Application blanks for the Merit Badge may be had on request at our general office by stating name and address of boy applying.

When requirements are complied with, the application blanks must be signed by the boy, his father, the ward president of Y. M. M. I. A., and the bishop.

A special Church merit certificate will be issued to the successful boy by the General Board. By remitting 50c he may also receive the Church Merit Badge.

In case of sickness credit will be given for attendance at meetings.

Scout Commissioner, Dr. John H. Taylor, spoke on "The Training of Leaders," dwelling on scout masters' associations, patrol leaders, records, examinations, scout promise, troop finances and standards for scout officials. The very interesting and valuable meeting came to a close by the congregation singing "Lend a helping hand." Prayer was offered by President William T. Jack of Cassia Stake.

DEMONSTRATION AT GYMNASIUM

In the evening a large number of people gathered at the Deseret Gymnasium the evening being devoted to a demonstration of a campfire gathering including a program of campfire songs, exercises, stories and talks. The speeches were made by National Committeeman, A. W. Ivins, Orson F. Whitney, B. H. Roberts and President Joseph F. Smith.

CAMP SCENE IN THE DESERET GYMNASIUM
Y. M. M. I. A. Demonstration, June, 1916

JOINT OFFICERS' MEETING AT THE ASSEMBLY HALL ON FRIDAY, JUNE 9, AT 10 A. M.

The hall was well filled, both in the gallery and in the auditorium. Singing, "High on the Mountain Top." Invocation by President Francis M. Lyman. Violin solo by Miss May Anderson. There were present on the stand a large number of the members of the General Boards of Young Men and Young Ladies. President Heber J. Grant presided and after the opening exercises read the slogan of the M. I. A.—"We stand for State- and Nation-wide Prohi-

A June 8, 1916, Boy Scout leader training meeting held at the Deseret Gym included talks by Church Scout Commissioner John H. Taylor, Waterloo Ward Scoutmaster Thomas George Wood, Bryant S. Hinckley, and other prominent Church Scouting leaders. Scouting specifics were discussed, and Scout songs and yells were demonstrated. Elder Heber J. Grant presided, and President Joseph F. Smith was in attendance at an evening campfire program.

Commemorating the organization of the Boy Scouts of America on a designated Sunday during February became known as "Scout Sunday" and was observed by Scout troops across the country in a variety of ways.

Within a few years Scouting was woven into Church curriculum and culture. Leadership training meetings were often held at the Deseret Gym in Salt Lake City. A special award, originally titled a "Church Merit Badge," was introduced and could be earned when a boy read the entire Book of Mormon and New Testament, regularly attended YMMIA and priesthood quorum meetings, and abstained from tobacco and liquor.

"Scout Sunday" originated in February 1914 to celebrate the anniversary of the Scouting organization. The YMMIA board set aside a Sunday evening in February as MIA Boy Scout evening. Suggestions in the *Improvement Era* included discussing Scouting aims and purposes. The January 1917 edition encouraged speakers to use the *Boy Scout Handbook* as a reference, and the young ladies of the YWMIA were invited to "co-operate . . . in making this a big event."

"The most important scout virtue is that of honor. Indeed, this is the basis of all scout virtues, and is closely allied to that of self-respect. When a scout promises to do a thing on his honor, he is bound to do it. The honor of a scout is a sacred thing, and cannot be lightly set aside or trampled on."

—*Handbook for Boys,* 1911

We Stand for Service to God and Country.

World War I MIA slogan

A Scout garden

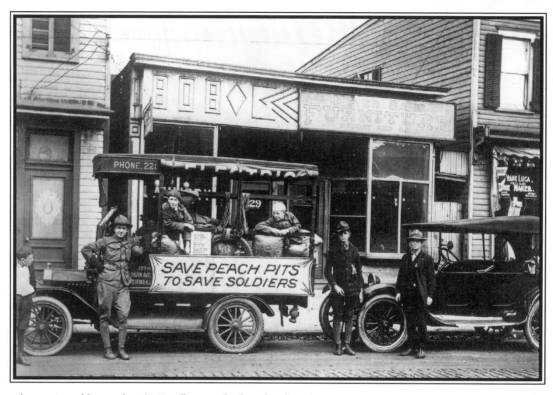

During World War I, Scouts across the country sold more than $355 million worth of war bonds and stamps,
delivered 300 million pieces of government literature, and filled 100 railroad cars with peach pits to be burned and used in gas mask filters.

World War I

The United States entered World War I on April 6, 1917. "Every Scout to Save a Soldier" became the national Boy Scout theme, and YMMIA boys and leaders were advised to also adopt this slogan. "Duty to country" took on new meaning for Scouts as thousands of boys actively sold Liberty Loan bonds and war stamps, distributed government literature, and grew gardens. Hundreds of acres of land across the United States—including Utah—were transformed into Scout gardens. Scouting and Church efforts progressed hand in hand as MIA leaders were asked to "lend their best endeavors to sell thrift stamps and war savings certificates."[21] MIA boys, ages sixteen through twenty-one, were encouraged to volunteer for the "U.S. Boys' Working Reserve," replacing men who had gone to war by working in machine shops, textile mills, and other industries. Extensive travel and activities were limited as youth and leaders devoted their time and energy to assisting the war effort.

Oscar A. Kirkham was a Scouter, musician, and Seventy. In 1912, he was appointed to the YMMIA board, and in April of 1919 became Scout Executive of the Salt Lake Boy Scout Council. He served the National Boy Scouts of America for over thirty-five years, attending numerous national and world jamborees as a morale officer. Elder Kirkham was sustained as a member of the First Council of the Seventy in 1941.

Scout Councils

Scouting continued to flourish throughout the Church in North America, with local LDS troops chartered under the direction of the YMMIA. It soon became apparent that the program was too large to be administered by one Church Scout commissioner. In 1919, Utah was divided into four Scout councils, and paid Scouting professionals were hired to assist in the program administration. This division of regions, troops, and activities made the growing program more manageable. As national membership grew, the development of councils became the standard for Scouting throughout the United States. LDS troops were encouraged to participate in all council activities, to use their facilities, and to assume their own full share of financial support for the essential work of the local Scout councils. Although the majority of Scout leaders were volunteers, it was clear that some paid professionals were needed to maintain the movement. However, national Boy Scout policy sought "to reduce to a minimum the machinery or organization."[22]

Scout councils were formed by calling together the leading men of the town or city. First Class councils were formed in urban areas, with paid commissioners or executives, while Second Class councils were formed in more rural areas and were managed through volunteer commissioners.

> **"The boy problem doesn't bother Oscar Kirkham. He is interested in the boy. And when you are interested in the boy the boy problem vanishes. . . . Whenever Oscar A. Kirkham comes to your stake or ward, round up your boys and let him touch them with his magic wand."**
> —Professor John H. Evans, *Improvement Era*, June 1913, 833

The first World Scout Jamboree was held in England in 1920. Scouts from over thirty countries gathered in a spirit of peace and goodwill, a powerful expression after the recent World War I. Oscar A. Kirkham attended the jamboree as Chief Morale Officer.

President Heber J. Grant and Oscar A. Kirkham with Utah Scouts at the 5th World Scout Jamboree, Netherlands, 1937

A Scout band on Temple Square, June 1925

CHAPTER 5

STANDARDIZED SCOUTING 1920–1939

President Heber J. Grant served on the YMMIA Board when the Church affiliated with the National Boy Scout organization.

I am happy to give the Boy Scout movement my full endorsement…. I was active in the promotion of this program. I feel that thousands of our boys have been helped in becoming good men by living up to the principles of the Boy Scout movement.

—President Heber J. Grant

Young men and leaders in the Church had enjoyed nearly ten years of official affiliation with the national Boy Scouts. Although obstacles had surfaced as the two organizations integrated, they were resolved and Church support for Scouting was still strong. A 1921 announcement from the YMMIA general board placed renewed emphasis on Church Scout troops being "organized and affiliated with the National Organization . . . and [making] use of their organization, programs, suits, badges, system of promotion, . . . privileges, advantages, recognitions or honors."[23]

Additionally, instead of dividing weekly MIA time between the Boy Scout and MIA programs, meetings were to be fully devoted to Scouting. Church leaders determined that religious training could naturally occur through Scouting activities.

Scout Bands

As the Scouting program grew, activities were coordinated and standardized within councils to build unity and provide recreation for the boys and troops. Scout bands were common in many towns and cities. Not only did bands march in parades, but they often gave concerts as well, performing a variety of music at various locations.

Junius Wells suggested forming a Scout band in Salt Lake City. After six months of hard work the boys made their first appearance at an MIA rally. A few days later, they played at the Granite Stake conference and then for the June 1920 MIA conference in the Tabernacle. On February 5, 1921, they marched in a street parade to commemorate the anniversary of the Boy Scout movement. Fifteen hundred boys participated in the parade.

Scout band banner presented by Junius Wells

SCOUT BAND CONCERT TABERNACLE TONIGHT

The people of this community will be given an opportunity this evening to show their appreciation of the Brigham Scout band and its able leader, C. C. Watkins. The band is composed of about fifty energetic boys, who are working hard to acquire a knowledge of music, and to perfect themselves in playing their respective instruments. They have made rapid progress, and are now able to furnish a real good brand of band music.

The band will give a concert at the tabernacle this evening, beginning at 7:30 o'clock, and following the concert, a grand ball will be given at the Academy of Music. The giving of these two entertainments has a two-fold purpose. First, to let the public know what progress the band is making, and second, to raise funds with which to purchase new music, needed instruments, and to meet the expense of the organization.

The boys are engaged in a worthy move, and should be given every support. They are a credit to Brigham city, and already demands for their music is coming from other cities. They are scheduled to play at Salt Lake city within the very near future.

The program at the tabernacle this evening is as follows:

OUR BOYS WILL SHINE TONIGHT _____ Vocal
JOLLIFICATION, March Ascher _____ Instrumental
PILGRIM CHORUS, Richard Wagner _____ Instrumental
JASMO, John N. Klohr _____ Instrumental
CARRY ME BACK TO OLD VIRGINNY, Bland ___ Vocal—Instrumental
ECHOES FROM THE SOUTH, John N. Klohr ___ Instrumental
SOUTHERN FIRE BRIGADE, March _____ Instrumental
HUMORESQUE—WHO'S NEXT?, H. Bellstedt, Jr. ___ Instrumental
THE STARS AND STRIPES FOREVER, Sousa ___ Instrumental
SAXAPHONE SOLO, Selected _____ Melvin B. Watkins
THE ADMIRAL OVERTURE, Edw. Russel _____ Instrumental
GOD'S COUNTRY, Vocal Ed Lee—THE STAR SPANGLED
BANNER _____ Instrumental

OFFICERS OF BAND

FRED J. HOLTON _____ PRESIDENT
N. CHRIS SIMONSEN _____ VICE-PRESIDENT
JOHN B. MATHIAS _____ SECRETARY AND TREASURER
E. W. WATKINS _____ DIRECTOR
C. C. WATKINS _____ BAND LEADER AND MANAGER

PATROL LEADERS AND ASSISTANTS

Fred Nelson	Isaac Hansen	Dwight Wright
Wallace Johnson	Vern Nelson	Floyd Grover
N. V. Watkins	Ijames Faulkner	Frank Hickenlooper
Lucius Johnson	Clifford Peterson	Howard Johnson
	Elmer Nelson	

MEMBERS

Glen Koford	Leroy Harper	Irvin Madsen
Wendell Hubbard	Ralph Jeppson	Theodore Demores
Dale Robbins	Lorenzo Vance	Forrest Kelley
Leonard Weed	Leon Christensen	Neville Tingey
LeGrand Wood	Earl Madsen	Opal Richardsen
Wesley Mitton	Leonda Hansen	Shorland Evans
Claud Jensen	Karl Josephson	Harding Horsley
George Williams	Delbert Knudson	Tom Harris
George Anderson	Irving Anderson	Jay Smith
Luther Robinette	William Tyson	Bernell Nelson
Emery Nichols	Clyde Earl	Wilmer Stokes
Kenneth Smith	Glen Wagstaff	Glen Sheffield
Delone Eliason	Clyde Madsen	Wayne Pulsipher
LeGrand Horsley	Herman Stayner	Barry Knudson
Waldo Forsgren	Hollis Lee	Owen Owens
Claudius Olsen	Wayne Sheffield	Don Peterson
Douglas Quayle	Raymond White	Rodney Simonsen
Glen Knudson	Denzel Forsgren	Wray Glenn
Grant Nelson	Dee J. Valentine	Farrel Lee
Carlyle Rich	Irwin Hansen	Alma Pratt
	Willard Christensen	

Meet the boys at the dance immediately following the concert at the Academy of Music.

A Brigham City Scout band,
Box Elder News, 1925

YMMIA leader Junius F. Wells suggested the formation of a Scout band in Salt Lake City. Rehearsals were first held in the old Deseret Gym, and then moved to the school rooms of the former tithing office. The band made so much noise that it was again moved to the rooms under the Barratt Hall, and finally received permission from the city commission to hold practices in the gymnasium of the public safety building, or police station.

"We need the national organization. We need it for the classification of Scouts, from tenderfoot to the Eagle Scout. We need its courts of honor; we need its system of merits and rewards; we need the 'national pull' that is found in these things.... Boy Scouting [is] a point of contact with our fellow citizens of the United States that is of great advantage to us.... Be friendly...in your attitude towards this great organization."

—Elder Brigham H. Roberts, First Council of the Seventy, general conference, Apr. 1922

Elder Brigham H. Roberts attended the March 1922 National Council Boy Scouts of America meeting in Chicago and reported in general conference.

1920s Troop 5 from Brigham City, Utah

"Scouting . . . takes the boy at the time of life when he is beset with the new and bewildering experience of adolescence, and diverts his thoughts therefrom to wholesome and worthwhile activities."
—*Improvement Era*, Apr. 1921, 55

Camp Kiesel, located 25 miles east of Ogden, Utah, was developed in 1926 by the Ogden Gateway Area Council. The camp was first operated by Council Scout Executive S. Dilworth Young, who was later ordained to the First Council of the Seventy.

"Scout is a word. Innumerable are its connotations. But to a boy it can have only one denotation. It means adventure—outdoor adventure."

—S. Dilworth Young, *Improvement Era,* July 1947, 435

"We firmly believe the permanent camp will become very popular in the future, for in no better way can boy friendships be made and cemented, and in such close and constant communion the scout learns more fully to realize his duty and obligation of service to his fellows."

—Arthur W. Sadler, Grant Stake recreation officer, Improvement Era, Nov. 1924, 34

Long-term Camps

"Outings" were an essential focus of Scouting, and extended campouts were vital to effectively teaching and implementing Scouting concepts. The advantages of organizing long-term camps for multiple troops soon became apparent. In August of 1924 the Salt Lake City Grant Stake conducted a week-long camp on the shores of Utah Lake. Stake leaders used the camp to coordinate the various activities of the ward troops. Scout councils soon acquired land and developed it into permanent camps with campsites, buildings, and facilities to support outdoor recreation.

"I became a Scout in 1922. . . . We met in our troop meeting on Tuesday evening. We were a noisy group as we assembled. Our Scoutmaster, Charlie Robinson, would blow his whistle, and we would all fall in line. We would raise our right arm to the square and repeat together the Scout oath. . . . It was something of a ritual each Tuesday. We did not think about it very deeply, but the words of that oath became fixed in our minds. They have remained with me through all of these years." —President Gordon B. Hinckley, Ensign, *May 1989, 46-47*

Scouts at Bryce Canyon

*Naturalist George Wharton James with Boy Scouts
at Zion Canyon, Utah, 1920*

Salt Lake Council officials arranged for a Boy Scout Caravan to take place July 10–18, 1920. The Utah State Automobile Association provided forty-five vehicles that carried approximately 250 participants over eight hundred miles in nine days. The October 1920 *Improvement Era* reported, "This journey, perhaps the most pretentious ever undertaken by Boy Scouts, will live a lifetime in the minds of those fortunate enough to have taken it." Participants all adopted a Native American name for the adventure and received tutelage on skills such as geography, geology, and citizenship at the hands of Church leaders like John H. Taylor and John D. Giles. They also had special guest instructors such as Dr. George Wharton James from California.

Boy Scouts on top of a natural bridge in southern Utah

"The boy scout program . . . —coupled with the spiritual work of our Church—is the best boy program yet devised, and it is our wish that a Boy Scout organization be effected and maintained in every M.I.A. Association in the Church in order that every lad of Scouting age may have this advantage of Scout-training."

—YMMIA General Superintendency,

Improvement Era, Apr. 1921

Trail Builder Log

Trail Builder Bandlo

Trail Builder Cap

Trail Builders

Scouting added an element of achievement and excitement to Church activities, effectively attracting and retaining twelve- and thirteen-year-old boys in YMMIA Scout troops. However, it became evident to Church leaders that the oldest Primary boys, ages ten and eleven, were not always as devoted to their Church activities. In 1925 the Trail Builders program was introduced for these boys, and they became Blazers, Trekkers, and Guides. Trail Builders earned emblems worn on a "bandlo" and wore a green hat with a picture of a pine tree. The program also had a special alphabet, a code, and a salute.

Three years later, in 1928, the Zion's Boys program was introduced for eight- and nine-year-old boys. Their red-and-white shield reminded them to "live purely" and "do right."[24] The Primary also developed achievement programs for older girls. In 1922 twelve- and thirteen-year-old girls were Seagulls, 1926 ten- and eleven-year-old girls were Bluebirds, and 1928 eight- and nine-year-old Primary girls were Zion's Girls. In 1929, the Home Builders groups were established with classes renamed Larks, Bluebirds, Seagulls, and Mi-kan-wees. In 1934, twelve- and thirteen-year-old girl classes became part of the YWMIA program.

"A boy is a man in a cocoon—you do not know what it is going to become—his life is big with many possibilities. He may make or unmake kings, change boundary lines between states, write books that will mold characters, or invent machines that will revolutionize the commerce of the world. . . . Be patient with the boys— you are dealing with soul-stuff. Destiny awaits just around the corner."

—Elbert Hubbard, American writer, as quoted in *Scouting in the LDS Church,* 1934

Primary Trail Builder boys prepare for Scouting.

Cubbing

The Boy Scouts of America also realized the need for a national program designed for boys younger than Scout age. After instigating a study and consulting with other youth organizations—including the Primary Association of the Church—the "Cubbing" program was developed. On August 1, 1929, the first Cub packs were organized to test the new program, and in 1933 Cubbing was introduced to Scout councils across the nation. However, it was not adopted by the LDS Church at this time. The new program was geared to the boy, his home, and his family.

The Vanguard Program

Boy Scout programs were enthusiastically accepted by most deacon- and teacher-age boys. After fifteen years of operating the national Scouting program within wards and branches, Church leaders became aware that many older boys were dropping out of Scout troops. In 1928, the Church officially named Scouting as the activity program for deacons and introduced the Vanguard Scout program for older boys, ages fifteen through eighteen.

Early Cub Scout

The 1931 *MIA Official Guide for Leisure and Recreation* **described desirable traits of a Scoutmaster:** "reverent," "will stick to the job and make it go," "clean morally and physically," "will register and re-register his boys," and "advance his troop." He is "a man who has the spirit of it." "He is in it because he loves [the Scouting program] and can see its possibilities."

Future Church President Howard W. Hunter was active in Boise, Idaho Scout Troop 13. After attending summer camp in 1922, he qualified for the Life Scout and Star Scout awards. President Hunter later recalled, "Only six more [merit badges] were required for the rank of Eagle Scout. The scouting magazine had carried stories of boys who had gained the rank of Eagle, but we were told there had not yet been one in Idaho. The race was on between Edwin Phipps of Troop 6 and me." By the next court of honor, both boys had earned twenty-one merit badges, but young Howard still lacked some required badges. Edwin received his Eagle award in March 1923, and Howard received his Eagle Scout award on May 11, 1923, the second Eagle Scout in Idaho. —Eleanor Knowles, Howard W. Hunter, 39-40

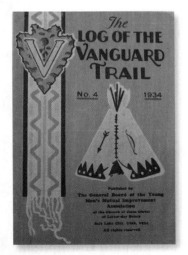

The Log of the Vanguard Trail
manual was published from 1931–1934
for Vanguard Scouts and leaders.

Elder George Albert Smith of the Council of the Twelve and General Superintendent of the YMMIA explained, "At fifteen, [a boy] may become a Vanguard where he is given a program of advanced Scouting. . . . At this age they are not satisfied to follow the commands of others, but aspire to leadership themselves. . . . The first novelty of Scouting has worn off, and they crave something new."[25]

Soon two troops were organized within wards—a Scout troop and a Vanguard troop. New program ideas were included in the March 1929 *Improvement Era*. Vanguard troops were to use the first Tuesday of each month for merit badge work, the second and fourth Tuesdays for developing their own social, recreational, and seasonal activities, and the third Tuesday to meet as individual patrols. Special emphasis was placed on earning the First Class, Star, Life, and Eagle Scout ranks.

Vanguard merit badges included astronomy, athletics, swimming, life saving, automobiling, aviation, horsemanship, salesmanship, reptiles, and other subjects.

Emery County Boy Scout Troop attending the 50th anniversary of the YMMIA celebrations in Salt Lake City, Utah, June, 1925

56

Explorer Scout

Definition: Vanguard
—An explorer or adventurer in new territory or unconquered regions

Explorer Scouts

The leadership opportunities and advanced activities of the Vanguard Scout program were effective in retaining older youth in the MIA Scouting organization. After five years of Church operation, the National Council requested permission to use the Vanguard curriculum as a basis for their advanced Scouting program. George Albert Smith readily agreed. In the new national program, older youth were called "Explorer Scouts."

Since the Explorer Scout program was in harmony with the Vanguard objectives, Church leaders willingly changed the YMMIA program name from *Vanguard* to *Explorer* on May 8, 1935. One month later, during the June 1935 MIA conference, a ceremony was held with Dr. Fisher of the National BSA council, and 7,000 LDS Vanguards were welcomed as Explorer Scouts into the BSA.

"The General Officers of the Young Women's Mutual Improvement Association are as concerned with the training of boys as they are with the training of girls. The lives of these young people parallel. They should march together to the same goal. Therefore we commend the Young Men's organization and all others who are engaged in this splendid work for boys. May their remarkable success be added upon ten-fold." —Ruth May Fox, YWMIA general president, *Improvement Era*, Feb. 1935, 99

The Scout learns his outdoor craft, the **Explorer** *uses* it in wider adventures.

Ruth May Fox
YWMIA general president

Boy Scout national encampment at Independence Rock, Wyoming, July 1930

Boy Scouts at Independence Rock encampment, July 1930

Celebrations and Anniversaries

Several Scouting and Church anniversaries were commemorated during the 1930s. April 1930 marked one hundred years since the organization of the Church. A new hymn for youth titled "Carry On" was introduced at the June conference and became the MIA theme song. In July of the same year, hundreds of Scouts from fifteen different states across America gathered at Independence Rock, Wyoming, in the first nationwide Scout encampment. Prominent Church and Scouting leaders, including Elder George Albert Smith of the Quorum of the Twelve Apostles and Chief Scout Executive James E. West, attended the event.

Church and Scouting leaders at Independence Rock, July 4, 1930
George Albert Smith, second from left; James E. West, third from right

A national jamboree was scheduled to commemorate the 25th anniversary of the Boy Scouts of America. The gala event was to be held in Washington, D.C., and drew the attention and support of the nation, including President Franklin D. Roosevelt. With great anticipation, several troops of LDS Scouts from Utah made preparations to participate in the memorable event. However, a polio epidemic forced the postponement of the jamboree until 1937.

Even though the jamboree was canceled, LDS troops still traveled east to visit Church history sites and tour New York; Washington, D.C.; and other cities. On their return trip west, these Scouts marked the Pony Express Trail as a service project.

Boy Scouts at the Hill Cumorah, 1935

Boy Scouts at Palmyra, New York, 1935

Boy Scouts on the Pony Express Trail, 1935

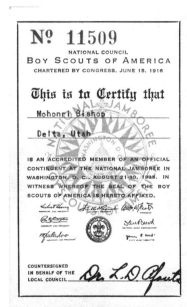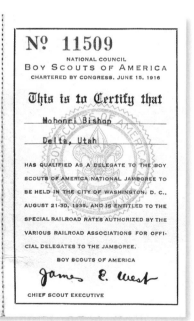

*Boy Scouts were issued cards that identified them as jamboree participants and
provided special discounts on railroad fares.*

Boy Scouts at Winter Quarters, 1935

Several national Scout groups formed in Germany, but no single organization obtained international recognition. On November 6, 1928, Church leaders from the German-Austrian and Swiss-German missions met with the leader of the German Späherbund (Scout group) in Leipzig to discuss the possibility of a Scouting organization and affiliation. The Scout Federation of Germany was successfully organized, and soon obtained international Scouting recognition. Of the 1000 enrolled members, approximately 600 were LDS Scouts.

World Scouting

The Scouting movement flourished around the world, and many countries established national organizations. The World Organization of the Scouting Movement (WOSM) was formed in 1922. Wherever possible, the Church established an affiliation with national Scouting organizations, similar to the partnership they had with the Boy Scouts of America. The February 1935 *Improvement Era* reported Latter-day Saint Scout troops in the following international locations: Austria, Australia, Belgium, Canada, Czechoslovakia, Denmark, England, France, Germany, Hawaii, Holland, Hungary, Ireland, Mexico, New Zealand, Norway, Samoa, Scotland, South Africa, Sweden, Switzerland, and the United States. Additionally, BSA troops were established in several areas outside of the United States, including Tonga and Colonia Juarez, Mexico.

George Albert Smith with international Scouts

Eagle Scouts in Colonia Juarez, Mexico

Boy Scout group in Nuku'alofa, Tonga

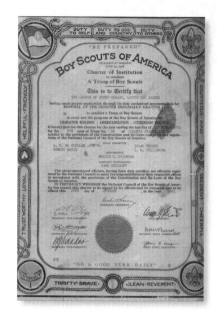

Colonia Juarez, Mexico Scout Charter

"The Church of Jesus Christ of Latter-day Saints is using the Boy Scout Program in a larger way than any other church in existence. . . . Your Church . . . has given a volunteer and a loyal leadership and support that is unequalled by any other religious body in America."

—Ray O. Wyland, Director of Education, National Organization, Boy Scouts of America

Improvement Era, Aug. 1928, 860-861

"Wherever the Church goes with its program for the temporal and eternal salvation of mankind, the Boy Scout program follows to assist in building manhood under whatever flag waves above the land in which the troop is organized."
—*Improvement Era,* Feb. 1935, 77

1938 Jubilee festivities included a parade and decorations on Main Street.

Jubilee decorations on Temple Square

By 1938

35,000

LDS Scouts were registered with the national BSA organization.

A Silver Anniversary

The silver anniversary of Scouting in the Church was a time to celebrate. Twenty-five years of affiliation had resulted in continued cooperation between the two organizations. National encampments and programs, dedicated leaders, and 35,000 registered LDS Scouts were reasons to commemorate. Impressive anniversary festivities were held in conjunction with the 1938 June MIA conference, including a jubilee signal fire on Ensign Peak, Salt Lake City. Activities culminated in a religious convocation in the Tabernacle on Sunday, June 2, with a notable gathering of Scouts and Explorers as well as Church and national Scouting leaders.

Cavalcade of Scouting program

THE CHILDREN'S FRIEND

SEPTEMBER · 1945

The IMPROVEMENT **ERA**

JUNE 1953

One of Life's Proudest Moments

The boy stands proudly before the entire Court of Honor while his mother, equally proud, nervously pins on the coveted Eagle. Truly, it's one of the high spots in a boy's life... and the lives of his parents.

The Eagle award is a symbol of the accomplishment of a goal. In a sense, your Beneficial Life policy is like that, too. You can feel a real sense of accomplishment when, after considerable study and counsel with your Beneficial agent, you successfully work out an insurance program that will give your family the financial protection they need — at a cost consistent with your income.

Over ¼ billion dollars of life insurance in force.

BENEFICIAL LIFE
Insurance Company

David O. McKay, Pres.   Salt Lake City · Utah

Church magazine covers often reflected a commitment to Scouting.

CHAPTER 6

GROWTH AND EXPANSION
1940–1969

We want our boys to be the finest Scouts in all the world. We should appropriate every good thing that scouting teaches us because it is a part of the gospel of Jesus Christ.

—President George Albert Smith

Elder George Albert Smith, then an Apostle, was appointed to the Boy Scout National Executive Board in 1931. He was the first Utahn to serve in this position.

The United States entered World War II on December 8, 1941, the day after Pearl Harbor was attacked by Japanese war planes. Walter W. Head, president of the Boy Scouts of America, and James E. West, Chief Scout Executive, immediately telegraphed President Roosevelt offering "the full and whole-hearted co-operation of our organization."[26] With a membership of 1,600,000 and troops in nearly every town or city, Boy Scouts could naturally perform grassroots services. In addition, they were trusted, clean-cut boys, readily recognized in their neighborhoods.

As war became a reality for young American boys, Church leaders were increasingly concerned about Latter-day Saint youth. In January 1942, a message was sent to stake and ward MIA leaders stating that "the greatest concern is . . . for our young people. They are the ones most vitally affected. . . . Our young men are being called from their homes to national service. . . . Many are bewildered; questions affecting their immediate future are constantly troubling them."[27] In accordance with wartime shortages of the day, June MIA conferences were cancelled, and general boards limited meetings and activities.

Church youth and leaders supported the war through ward and stake MIA activities. Patriotic programs were held and welfare gardens, first aid, food conservation, nursing, and other projects were conducted. Boy Scout troops organized drives to collect valuable products such as rubber and paper and performed other good turns. In addition, Scouts served in official capacities, distributing information and fliers through their communities.

"I need not tell you that I am proud of the record the Boy Scouts of America achieved during the war. Frankly, I knew they would come through. . . . [It] proves that you can depend on the Boy Scouts."[28] —General Dwight D. Eisenhower

1943 Scoutmaster membership card

Boy Scouts assisted with the unveiling of the This Is the Place *monument, July 1947.*

Pioneer Centennial

Utah was spared much of the devastation of World War II. After the war ended, young men and fathers returned to their homes, and Church and Scouting activities resumed their normal pace. The centennial of the pioneers entering the Salt Lake Valley and the thirty-seventh anniversary of the Boy Scouts of America were commemorated in 1947.

A Pioneer Centennial Scout Camp was held during July at Fort Douglas in Salt Lake City for a "five-day demonstration of the values of the scouting program." The program included "a gigantic campfire; Scouts on parade . . . with thirty bands; a tabernacle program, . . . and participation in the 'This Is The Place' monument dedication."[29] In a respectful recognition of the age-gap between older and younger boys, a separate camp was held for Explorer Scouts.

Older Scouts

The successful training of older young men continued to develop within the Church. "Exploring into Manhood," a guide for MIA Explorers, was published by the YMMIA general board in the 1940s, reemphasizing the importance of administering the program with "dynamic leadership," and under the "direct responsibility" of Church leaders.

The Church established the Explorer Scout Deseret Recognition award in 1945 to honor religious service. Because the word *deseret* is understood to mean *honeybee*, the award in part represented the recipient's hard work and courage. The award was earned by completing goals in Aaronic Priesthood activity, reading the scriptures or other Church literature, fulfilling leadership responsibility, giving service, studying Church or family history, and participating in a public performance through music, speaking, or sharing. Once earned, Explorers became members of the Deseret Recognition Club.

Stake and ward budgets initially covered expenses for their respective Scouting units and local Scout councils. In 1947, the Boy Scout national organization adopted a fundraising plan that included the entire community. In a letter dated May 28, 1948, Presiding Bishop LeGrand Richards and MIA General Superintendent George Q. Morris wrote, "In the spirit of loyalty . . . we join with other community leaders to provide finances to carry on the Scouting program efficiently and with credit to the Church and the Boy Scouts of America." Church members were now encouraged to support local council fundraising efforts outside of their individual ward or branch budget.

In 1949, a national revision in BSA membership policy registered all Scouts, fourteen years of age and older, as Explorers. This change integrated the entire teachers quorum into the Exploring program.

Church Explorer posts were encouraged to hike the "Pioneer Trail," 37 miles from Henefer, Utah, through East Canyon to the "This Is the Place" Monument. The purpose of the activity was to instill an appreciation for pioneer heritage in the youth.

"We have through a combination of scouting and Aaronic Priesthood work, the finest program for boyhood that this world knows anything about. I am convinced of that."

—Elder Ezra Taft Benson, *Improvement Era,* Sep. 1948, 558

The twenty-four carat gold Deseret Recognition pin displayed images of a beehive (industry), temple spires (spiritual strength), and mountains (the outdoors).

Elder Ezra Taft Benson, an Apostle of the Church, succeeded President George Albert Smith on the National Executive Board of the Boy Scouts of America in 1949. Pictured here with his two sons.

"There is no other program in all the world that has been so effective in developing the character of boys as Scouting. . . . We should dedicate ourselves to . . . the boys who are growing up under our care, so that we may have their companionship not only in life but through all eternity."
—President George Albert Smith, April 1930

Mormon Relationships

Good relationships were an important ingredient in the continued affiliation of the Church and the Boy Scouts of America. As Scouting grew in both organizations, constant communication between key leaders was vital. President George Albert Smith had served on the Boy Scout National Executive Board since 1931, sharing the desires and opinions of the Church with other national volunteers. Elder Ezra Taft Benson, a member of the Quorum of the Twelve Apostles, was appointed to the National Executive Board in 1949, replacing President Smith.

In the fall of 1950, Elder Benson proposed a national Mormon Relationships Service, similar to the Protestant, Jewish, and Catholic services already in place. In agreement with his suggestion, the Executive Board established the job of Director of Mormon Relationships as a nationally appointed Boy Scout assignment. The national position was filled by mutual agreement between the Church and national leaders, and the individual was required to be a priesthood bearer. Responsibilities would include interpreting and promoting the program of the Boy Scouts of America to the Church, and also interpreting the Church, its organization, policies, and standards to the Boy Scouts of America. D.L. "Lou" Roberts was the first BSA professional to be appointed as Director of Mormon Relationships.

President David O. McKay also established a General Church Scouting Relationships Committee to "set policies, approve program activities and in general extend the influence of the Boy Scout program throughout the Church."[30]

Local councils were also encouraged to form committees and ensure optimal communication between the Church and the BSA on a local level. By 1966, fifty-four local Scout councils had organized Mormon Relationships Committees.

"Since scouting emphasizes a boy's 'duty to God,' it has great appeal to the Church as an integral part of the program to make religion vital in the lives of boys."
—D. "Lou" Roberts,
YMMIA General Board,
Director of Mormon Relationships,
Improvement Era, June 1953, 470

A General Church Scouting Relationships Committee was appointed October 24, 1951. Committee members included President David O. McKay and Elders Ezra Taft Benson, Mark E. Petersen, LeGrand Richards, and others. General Primary leaders eventually served on the committee as well.

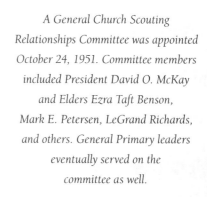

"When a boy reaches his eleventh birthday, he can take his Tenderfoot test and register [as a Scout]. From then on he can advance rapidly in the program, wear the uniform, and do the other things an older Scout can do except attend regular evening meetings."
—*Improvement Era*, Apr. 1951, 235

Elder Mark E. Petersen with eleven-year-old Scouts

"You cannot divorce Church work from scouting. Church work and scouting are identical so far as the scouting program is concerned."

—Elder Mark E. Petersen, *Improvement Era*, Feb. 1951, 98

Eleven-Year-Old Scouts

The 1949 national membership policy change lowered the introductory Boy Scout age from twelve to eleven, aligning the Boy Scouts of America with international Scouting standards. However, the age change posed a problem for the Church, since it wasn't until a boy turned twelve that he was ordained a deacon and became a member of Church Scouting programs.

After discussion and prayer among members of the Primary general board, Sister Adele Howells, Primary general president, recommended to the First Presidency that eleven-year-old Scouting be conducted under the jurisdiction of the YMMIA. The First Presidency agreed. Scout troops were instructed to hold two weekly meetings: an evening meeting in conjunction with MIA activities, and another weekday meeting for eleven-year-old boys. Eleven-year-old Scouts would attend the daytime Scout meeting and their weekly Primary meetings, while older boys would attend both the daytime meeting and their evening MIA Scout meetings.

The two-meeting system offered several advantages. The first was the outdoor benefit, since daytime meetings provided more opportunity for activities in the open air. The second advantage was in leadership, since an eleven-year-old Scout leader could be called as an assistant Scoutmaster of the ward troop. Eleven-year-old Scouts were referred to as "Guides" from their Primary class name, or "Candidate Scouts," because they were admitted into the troop without achieving a specified rank.

Scouting Comes to the Primary Association

Despite the eagerness of young boys to join Scouting, dividing the responsibility between the Primary and the YMMIA proved complex. In May 1952, newly sustained Primary general president LaVern Parmley met with the First Presidency and the Presiding Bishopric to discuss the problem. President David O. McKay directed Sister Parmley to adapt the Primary curriculum to include Scouting along with priesthood preparation, and placed the entire responsibility for eleven-year-old boys under Primary leadership.

Chief Scout Executive Joseph A. Brunton Jr. met with Primary leaders in Salt Lake City to help organize the Scouting program for eleven-year-old Primary boys. Cub Scout den mothers had been recognized within the BSA since 1936; however, women had never officially registered as Boy Scout leaders. At the request of the Primary general board, Mr. Brunton provided authorization for women to serve in Boy Scouting even though they could not be registered, wear uniforms, or receive leadership awards. Primary Scout leaders—both women and men—were responsible for preparing boys to receive the priesthood and achieve the rank of Second Class Scout. A day-time camp program for Guide Patrol members was introduced during the April 1966 general conference.

President David O. McKay and Elder Ezra Taft Benson welcome an eleven-year-old boy into Scouting.

"I would like to say that where we find the best Aaronic Priesthood work, we find the best scouting being done. . . . Every principle of scouting is a principle of the restored gospel of the Lord Jesus Christ. There is no question about it."
—Bishop Joseph L. Wirthlin, *Improvement Era*, Feb. 1951, 87

The Primary Guide class was renamed the Guide Patrol.

In 1969, Primary general president LaVern Parmley became the first LDS woman to serve on a national Scout committee. Subsequent Primary general presidents have also served on national Scout committees by virtue of their calling.

Officially established as Cubbing, the program was renamed Cub Scouting in 1945.

"Cub Scouting is a potent and effective part of the youth program of the Church and must have the enthusiastic support of the priesthood and Primary workers. The Latter-day Saint belief in the eternal nature of the family places special emphasis on the value of this home-centered program."

—President David O. McKay, Circular, Dec. 19, 1960

Cub Scouting

President McKay also asked Sister Parmley to establish Cub Scouting within the Primary Association. The official Church announcement was made by President McKay on December 31, 1952. Members and leaders were encouraged to cooperate in the "worthy objectives of the program" and to "willingly respond and help." In addition, it was emphasized that "a boy who begins his scouting experience under the sponsorship of the Church in Cub Scouting automatically . . . completes his Scouting and Exploring in the YMMIA."[31] Cub Scouting was the final link in providing a complete Church Scouting program for LDS boys ages eight through eighteen.

Cub Scouting was organized under the direction of the Primary, with leaders called by the bishopric and meetings conducted in neighborhoods and homes. Wards formed Cub Scout packs and committees, and the newly approved program grew rapidly. Within the first year of adopting Cub Scouting, the Church established 114 packs.

Initially, Cub Scout dens across the nation were led by Den Mothers, while Den Dads served on the Cub Scout committee. With the growth of Cub Scouting, the National Executive Board soon recognized that Cub Scout needs could be better served if women were directly involved in committees, including the National Cub Scout Committee. In 1969 Primary general president LaVern Parmley was invited to serve on the National Cub Scout Committee. BSA National President Robert Reneker's wife, Elizabeth, was also invited to serve, thus making both of them the first female members in a national capacity.

Women were eventually allowed to register as Boy Scout troop and Cub Scout pack commissioners in 1973, and as Cubmasters in 1976. In 1988 women could hold every position in Scouting, including Webelos Leader and Scoutmaster.

When Sister LaVern Parmley was instructed by President David O. McKay to establish both Scouting and Cub Scouting within the Primary Association, she remarked that she felt she was "going up against a stone wall." President McKay responded, "The wall may seem insurmountable but . . . there may be a hidden ladder."[32] Sister Parmley forged ahead in effectively implementing both programs within the Church. Her years of dedication to Scouting demonstrated that she had indeed discovered the "hidden ladder" mentioned by President McKay.

CUB SCOUTING
in the Church of Jesus Christ of Latter-day Saints

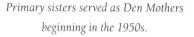

Primary sisters served as Den Mothers beginning in the 1950s.

"Great ideals and principles do not live from generation to generation just because they are right, not even because they have been carefully legislated. Ideals and principles continue from generation to generation only when they are stamped on the hearts of children as they grow up."

—LaVern Parmley, Primary general president, 1951-1974, as cited by the Boy Scouts of America

"I am convinced that the program, the goals, the purposes, and the Boy Scouts of America are worthy of the active support and involvement of women everywhere."
—Belle S. Spafford, Relief Society general president, Relief Society Magazine, *Apr. 1970, 256*

Exploring

Sock hops, drive-in movies, and rock and roll music were trademark trends of the 1950s. A post–World War II society offered an increased array of career opportunities for teenage youth. In keeping with the times, the Explorer program was expanded to include a wider variety of activities. Special interest Explorer posts were organized to appeal to all young men—those who had and those who hadn't been Boy Scouts—and to help them establish sound ideals for their future lives. In addition, a new uniform and logo were created. Areas of emphasis included vocational, service, outdoor, citizenship, and religious activities. The Church fully embraced the new Exploring program, which went into effect in December 1958. In an effort to differentiate between teacher- and priest-age boys, young men ages seventeen and eighteen were known as Ensign-Explorers, or Ensigns, and registered as Explorers.

On January 8, 1954, the Duty to God award was announced for young men who had faithfully fulfilled their religious duties. Requirements included at least four years of participation in the Aaronic Priesthood, attendance at Sunday School, and activity in the YMMIA as a Scout or Explorer. The award image depicted the Salt Lake Temple.

Sister Parmley with Scouts at Colorado Springs, Colorado National Jamboree, 1960

The Duty to God award was enhanced in 1968 with the Duty to God Trail program and included yearly recognition pins, with the first pin earned upon completion of Primary. The award image depicted Joseph Smith and Oliver Cowdery receiving the Aaronic Priesthood.

1954 Duty to God award

Silver Explorer award patch

In 1959, the Explorer program was renamed *Exploring*. Explorer units were referred to as *posts*. The Boy Scout program was renamed *Scouting*.

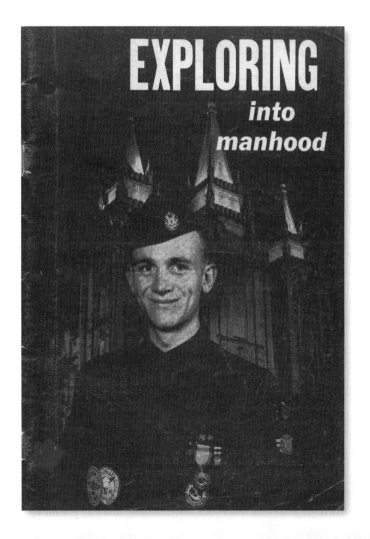

EXPLORING *into manhood*

At the end of 1959, the Church sponsored

943

Cub Scout packs,

2443

Boy Scout troops, and

1798

Explorer Posts.

*"It is the desire of the First Presidency that Latter-day Saint boys have the full advantage of the
Scouting program . . . [and] have this experience in units sponsored by the Church, under the direction of
Church leaders, and according to Church policies and standards."* —President David O. Mckay, Circular, Dec. 19, 1960

In Support of Scouting

Scouting statistics shared in February of 1960 portrayed the growth and power of the fifty-year old organization. Forty-five trillion good turns had theoretically been performed by thirty-three million boys and men living up to the national slogan, "Do a Good Turn Daily." Membership had passed the five million mark, with 125,000 units sponsored by 85,000 local institutions. The Eagle Scout rank was achieved by approximately fourteen of every thousand Scouts.

In an effort to participate in and assist the exploding national program, a course of study was established at Brigham Young University to train Scouting professionals. A February 5, 1965, letter from the First Presidency urged stake presidents to encourage young men to "investigate the possibilities of service in the field of professional Scouting."[33] In subsequent years, the Youth Leadership Department was expanded to include several faculty members and a curriculum offering over twenty classes on membership, camping, Cub Scouting, Boy Scouting, Exploring, and other related topics. Management concepts for additional nonprofit organizations were taught as well. Even if program graduates were not professionally employed by the Boy Scouts, it was anticipated that they would still have a greater understanding of the Scouting program in future volunteer Church assignments.

The Church emphisized the fact that "an effective communication link between the National Scouting program and the Church Scouting program is more important than ever."[34] To aid in communication and correlation, the second counselor in each ward bishopric was assigned to act as the Scouting coordinator within the ward. His title was Institutional Representative, and he was the ward's direct contact with the local Boy Scout district. He also worked with quorum advisers and Scouting leaders to coordinate and support activities, and helped to unify Scouting between the Primary and the YMMIA.

Stakes also formed Scouting committees. The committee chairman was a counselor to the stake president, with four high councilors serving on the committee. A member of each stake presidency was appointed to serve on the local Scout council board.

The Church Scouting Committee comprised the Presiding Bishop, his two counselors, the YMMIA Superintendency, and the Primary general president. In addition, the Director of Mormon Relationships continued his important role as a liaison between the two organizations.

> "The ideals and objectives of the Boy Scouts, as expressed in the Scout Oath, Law and Motto, [are] completely in harmony with the belief and practices of the Church. . . . By adopting the Boy Scout program, the Church [has] the help of this popular youth organization to enlist the interest of all its boys in its youth activities."
> —*Boy Scouting in the Young Men's Mutual Improvement Association,* 1968, 3

Brother Burton F. Brasher, high councilor from the Salt Lake City Jordan North Stake and later a member of the Young Men general board, attended the first Mormon Leaders Training Conference at Philmont Scout Ranch in 1963: "I immediately signed up and received permission . . . to represent our stake." On the final day of the conference, Elder Delbert L. Stapley of the Quorum of the Twelve and YMMIA Superintendent G. Carlos Smith, came to Philmont and asked the participants for feedback. "We told them it was a 'good conference.' They explained that our assignment was to 'go back to our own stake and preach the gospel about Scouting.'"

Philmont Scout Ranch is the premier High Adventure Base of the Boy Scouts of America. Located in northern New Mexico, the base offers more than 214 square miles of wilderness for backpacking treks, horseback cavalcades, and training and service programs to both Scouts and leaders. The land and ranch buildings were gifted to the Boy Scouts of America in 1938 and 1941 by oilman Waite Phillips, who observed, "The only things we keep permanently are those we give away." The ranch buildings were converted into a training center, and Scout leaders participate in conferences with their families. Nearly 30,000 participants attend Philmont Scout Ranch each year.

Philmont

General Church leaders desired that stake leaders fully understand the coordination of Scouting and priesthood functions, so they initiated a "Mormon Leaders Training Conference" in 1963. The week-long course was held at Philmont Scout Ranch in northern New Mexico. Church leaders—with BSA assistance—trained stake presidents and counselors in the functions of the Scouting program as they correlated with the work of the priesthood. Fifty stake presidents and other Church leaders participated in the first conference. Primary general presidencies and board members also eventually attended Philmont LDS conferences as faculty members, teaching principles of Cub Scouting and Eleven-year-old Scouting to stake leaders.

Philmont LDS Conference faculty members, 1965

The Philmont priesthood conference had several different names from 1963 through 2013 including, "Mormon Leaders Training Conference," "Mormon Scouting Workshop Conference," "Seminar on Aaronic Priesthood and Scouting," and "Priesthood Leadership Conference on Scouting."

In 1963, Elders David Allen and Thomas Hunsaker, fulltime missionaries in the North German Mission, were released from their proselyting duties and called by European Mission president Elder Ezra Taft Benson to establish an affiliation with the National German Scouting program and reorganize Scouting in German Church units. Elders pictured here in uniform with LDS Scouts, Düsseldorf, Germany.

International Church Scouting

Church leaders continued to emphasize affiliation with national Scouting organizations everywhere. The Vanguard program (different from the 1928 older Scout program) was initiated in 1957 for Church units outside of the United States where no national Scouting program was available. Membership was open to all youth ages twelve to fourteen, including those who were not Church members. Curriculum included activities, advancement, achievement, and spiritual growth. A decade later, in 1969, the MIA Scout achievement program replaced the previously used international Vanguard program.

Events and Commemorations

Half a century had passed since the official affiliation of the Church and the Boy Scouts of America. An anniversary program titled "The Golden Years of Scouting in the Church" was presented in the Salt Lake Tabernacle during the 1963 June MIA conference.

An International Explorer Conference was held in August at BYU. Approximately 3,700 LDS young men and leaders from twenty-nine states; Washington, D.C.; and five foreign countries attended the powerful Scout and priesthood leadership training. Church leaders in attendance at the 1963 Explorer Conference included President Henry D. Moyle, President Joseph Fielding Smith, and Elders Harold B. Lee, Ezra Taft Benson, and N. Eldon Tanner. Explorer conferences were held every two years from 1963 through 1971. The BSA started hosting Explorer Conferences in 1971, and Church leaders then encouraged LDS Scouts to attend these national events.

Boy Scouts listen to President McKay on the radio.

On February 8, 1966, the Church held a special program of rededication to Scouting. The program featured a radio broadcast entitled "Recommittal 1966." The impressive ceremony was conducted by President David O. McKay, then ninty-two years of age. His address was also presented via radio to "Scouts and Scouters of the Church in Canada" on February 22, 1966.

"Scout Sunday" continued as a yearly commemoration in the Church, with specific program instructions provided by the First Presidency and Presiding Bishopric to bishops and branch presidents. A circular dated October 21, 1968 suggested that the 1969 Scout Sunday program include songs, prayers, a Cub Scout chorus, and talks on such subjects as "Love of Country" and "How My Experiences in Scouting Have Helped Me in My Priesthood Responsibilities."

A Canadian–U.S. LDS Scout Encampment was held July 27-August 1, 1966, at Farragut, Idaho. Over 3,500 LDS boys and leaders from Western Canada and from the states of Oregon, Washington, Montana, and Idaho attended.

1966 Farragut Conference

Elder Thomas S. Monson was appointed to the National Executive Board in 1969, succeeding Elder Ezra Taft Benson.

Welcome sign for the 1966 Encampment at Farragut State Park, Idaho

For the Strength of Youth was first published in 1965.

It is important for our boys to begin their Scouting experience when they are young. . . . The Cub Scout motto cannot help but influence them in other areas of their lives."

—*Dwan J. Young, Primary general president, 1980–1988,* Church News, *Feb. 20, 1988*

CONSOLIDATION AND CHANGES 1970–1999

A young man who understands and is fully committed to the great principles of the Scout Law

has his feet firmly planted on a path that can lead to a happy and constructive life.

—President Spencer W. Kimball

President Spencer W. Kimball

A new decade brought changes to both the Boy Scouts of America and the LDS Church. Baby boomers grew older, and national Scouting membership dropped. In addition, activities such as Little League started interfering with Scouting participation. In an attempt to rejuvenate the program, a new *Boy Scout Handbook* was published in 1970 with fewer outdoor skill requirements.

Church membership grew, including many more members outside of the United States. Steps were taken during the 1970s to more closely correlate Scouting with the Aaronic Priesthood programs of the Church. Church manuals emphasized that the Aaronic Priesthood and Scouting programs were now one. Priests, formerly called Ensign-Explorers, were renamed Explorers and placed under the direction of the bishop. Deacons continued as Boy Scouts.

A new Church program titled Venturing was introduced for teacher-age young men in 1971. These boys were referred to as Venturers within the Church but were registered as Explorers with the BSA. The program allowed them to continue their Scouting advancement as well as serve in junior leadership positions for the younger Boy Scout troop.

The BSA Exploring program had evolved to include posts sponsored by special interest groups such as police officers and fire stations. Explorer Posts focused on a variety of diverse fields such as engineering, computers, auto mechanics, medical careers, law enforcement, aviation, theater, and basketball. Although Church Explorer Posts continued as all-male groups, national membership policy changes in 1971 allowed girls to register as Explorers.

President Spencer W. Kimball received the Silver World Award on April 2, 1977, during the general priesthood session of conference. This BSA recognition is presented to an individual who has provided extraordinary service to youth on an international scale.

Explorers around a campfire

Explorers, 1970

The Explorer Code

As an Explorer—

I believe that America's strength lies in
her trust in God and in the courage
and strength of her people.

I will, therefore, be faithful in my religious
duties and will maintain a personal sense of
honor in my own life.

I will treasure my American heritage and
will do all I can to preserve and enrich it.

I will recognize the dignity and worth
of my fellow men and will use fair play
and good will in dealing with them.

I will acquire the Exploring attitude that seeks
the truth in all things and adventure
on the frontiers of our changing world.

The Explorer Motto

Our best today—for a better tomorrow.

President Spencer W. Kimball with an Explorer

Church Awards and Recognitions

The Duty to God award had originally included requirements related to Scouting, including being a registered member of the BSA and achieving the rank of Star Scout. However, with a growing worldwide population, the award became solely a priesthood recognition in 1977, with award requirements designed to fit the needs of young priesthood holders everywhere.

The Church also created an On My Honor Scouting award specifically for Scouts and Explorers registered with the BSA, and the Faith in God award was introduced in 1978 for Cub Scouts. These recognitions provided an opportunity for boys to earn a Scouting award with a Church emphasis. Achievement records were printed in many languages, emphasizing the Church's worldwide nature.

In an effort to recognize LDS troops that were best utilizing the Scouting program, in 1973 the Church named the "Top 50 Troops in the Church." These troops were selected by the Deacon's Committee of the APMIA (Aaronic Priesthood MIA). In 1973, "the top troops were named [on] June 23 at a special honor assembly held after the session of the Deacon's Department during June Conference."[35]

Duty to God, 1977

On My Honor, 1977

Faith in God, 1978

"Being true to Scout principles will help [a young man] in forming a companionship with his Heavenly Father that will strengthen all the other relationships and aspects of his life."

—President Spencer W. Kimball, *Ensign*, May 1977

The Guide Patrol was renamed the Blazer Scout Patrol in the 1970s.

In 1972 the Primary developed a Scouting program to be used in nations where national Scouting charters were unobtainable.

Churchwide Correlation

Ward and stake budget changes were made in 1974, and instead of allocating funds for Boy Scout financial support, Church members were encouraged to participate in the Sustaining Membership Enrollment (SME) of local councils. The Presiding Bishopric suggested that "every family" with a Scouting member be "invited to participate" in "support of this worthwhile program."[36]

From 1974 to 1977, General Authority leadership of the Church's youth was placed under the jurisdiction of the Presiding Bishopric, with Victor L. Brown serving as Presiding Bishop. The name MIA was discontinued, and the youth organizations were referred to as Young Men and Young Women. In 1977, a general Young Men presidency was organized with Neil D. Schaerrer as president. In 1980 the Church took a historic step towards emphasizing the importance of family time when Church meetings were consolidated within a three-hour Sunday block of time.

National Changes

Scouting leaders placed a new focus on revising the program to once again more closely resemble Baden-Powell's original outdoor curriculum. In 1979, the *Boy Scout Handbook* was rewritten, and an effort to return to traditional American values was emphasized. These changes soon resulted in a steady increase in membership.

Retaining older youth was a constant priority of the national council, as well as LDS Church leaders. In 1974, several volunteer LDS Scout leaders developed a curriculum for youth ages fourteen and fifteen. Their efforts eventually resulted in "Varsity Scouting." Its purpose was to allow older boys the opportunity to continue on the Eagle Scout trail, yet still participate in more advanced activities.

After piloting the program in several Utah councils, Varsity Scouting was officially adopted by the Church on September 23, 1983, for teacher-age young men. President Ezra Taft Benson made the announcement, reaffirming that the new program would be a "great new resource to strengthen the young men" and would help them "continue toward achievement of the rank of Eagle Scout."[37] A year later, Varsity Scouting became a national BSA program, although it was used mainly in Church units.

The national Exploring program was replaced in 1998 with a new program, Venturing. It closely resembled the Exploring program of the 1940s and 1950s. Career-awareness Explorer Posts were now integrated into a newly created Learning for Life department, which coordinated all BSA in-school programs and focused on life skills as well as character, leadership, and citizenship. All LDS Explorers joined the Venturing program. Venturing quickly became the fastest-growing program in the BSA.

Varsity Scouting used sports terminology. Youth were organized into teams rather than troops, with a team captain. Leaders were Coaches instead of Scoutmasters.

The Church magazines were restructured in 1971. The New Era *replaced the* Improvement Era.

President Ezra Taft Benson received the Bronze Wolf at the Diamond Jubilee Commemoration in the Salt Lake Tabernacle, 1985.

President Ezra Taft Benson with Scouts during the 1977 National Scout Jamboree

Jamborees and Celebrations

The Scouting tradition of jamborees, or "joyful, noisy gathering,"[38] was initiated by Baden-Powell to develop friendship and goodwill among Scouts. Since the first world Scout jamboree held in England in 1920, and the national jamboree held in Washington, D.C., in 1937, Church leaders had developed a steady tradition of support and involvement in these monumental Scout gatherings. Prophets, apostles, and other General Authorities regularly attended and participated, along with numerous LDS Scouts.

Aside from national and international disasters—such as the polio outbreak of 1935 and World War II—jamborees were held every four years. World Scout jamborees were located around the world, while the BSA national jamborees alternated in places such as Washington, D.C.; Valley Forge, Pennsylvania; Colorado Springs, Colorado; and Irvine Ranch, California. National Scout jamborees found a permanent home at Fort A.P. Hill, Virginia, in 1981, and national jamborees were held there approximately every four years through 2010.

During the 1973 National Scout Jamboree, LDS Scouts received a card detailing their responsibilities as Scouts and priesthood holders.

Boy Scouts at the 1977 National Scout Jamboree

The 1973 National Scout Jamboree was held simultaneously at Morraine State Park, Pennsylvania, and Farragut State Park, Idaho. Approximately six thousand LDS Scouts attended at the jamboree sites with their leaders. Sixteen Melchizedek Priesthood holders served as LDS chaplains, directed by Elder Robert L. Backman, President of the Aaronic Priesthood MIA. Presiding Bishop Victor L. Brown attended meetings at Jamboree West, while Bishop H. Burke Peterson presided at services at Jamboree East.

"By living the Scout Oath and preparing for the oath and covenant of the Melchizedek Priesthood, you are truly preparing yourselves to serve God, your fellow man, your family, and your community. Taking the Scout Oath is a sacred trust endorsed by the First Presidency."
—Elder Vaughn J. Featherstone, Young Men General President, 1985-90, *New Era*, Feb. 2006, 10-13

75 Years of Scouting commemoration, Tabernacle on Temple Square, Feb. 8, 1985

Support for Scouting

Church leaders were also closely involved with the National Executive Board and committees. Members of the Primary and Young Men general presidencies and their boards served on national Scouting committees by virtue of their Church callings. The BSA National Annual meetings were held in Salt Lake City during May 1984. At a special *Music and the Spoken Word* program on May 24, the Mormon Tabernacle Choir showcased the Scout hymn, "On My Honor."

On February 8, 1985, 75 years of Scouting in America was commemorated with a special broadcast originating in the Tabernacle on Temple Square. Live satellite transmission to stake centers throughout the United States included addresses by President Gordon B. Hinckley of the First Presidency; President Ezra Taft Benson and Elder Thomas S. Monson of the Council of the Twelve; Elder Robert L. Backman, then serving as Young Men General President; and Sanford N. McDonnell, President of the Boy Scouts of America.

Priesthood leadership training for stake leaders continued each summer at Philmont Scout Ranch. During 1986 and 1987 Aaronic Priesthood Explorer Instructor Training Conferences were also held for Explorer-age young men under the direction of the Young Men General Presidency. The purpose of these conferences was to train young men in priesthood and Scouting leadership skills.

Donated funds and labor helped to build an LDS chapel at Philmont Scout Ranch in 1986. Each summer, daily sacrament services are provided for LDS participants. A leaded glass window at the front of the chapel portrays the Savior, a fleur-de-leis, and iris blooms and was designed by LDS artist Peter Fillerup. Brother Fillerup also created a bronze statue, *Duty to God*, which depicts a Scout holding a Book of Mormon. Sales from a limited edition of the sculpture helped to fund the one-room building.

LDS Chapel at Philmont

Peter Fillerup's statue *Scouting, Road to Manhood* stands near the Philmont Registration building, as well as at the National Scouting Museum in Irving, Texas.

"One of the best things that happens in Cub Scouting is family involvement."

—Patricia P. Pinegar, Primary general president, 1994-1999, *Church News*, Feb. 24, 1996

"I am thankful to have tools such as Scouting that we can use to help teach boys worthwhile character traits and help them develop skills and self-esteem, all while having fun."
—Michaelene P. Grassli,
Primary general president, 1988-1994,
Church News, *Feb. 19, 1994*

Anniversary Patch

The year 1988 marked the 75th anniversary of Scouting in The Church of Jesus Christ of Latter-day Saints. A special patch—including images of both Baden-Powell and the angel Moroni—was created to commemorate the anniversary.

The following November, Scouting units from across the United States performed a well-orchestrated good turn by participating in the first national "Scouting for Food" drive. The cooperative effort involved Cub Scouts and Boy Scouts distributing plastic bags door to door, which individuals and families then filled with nonperishable food. These bags were later collected by Varsity Scouts and Explorers. Church Leaders recognized that the activity accomplished "a priesthood purpose"[39] and encouraged Church units to participate. Sixty-five million containers of food were collected across the country.

Scouting for food

Young Men General Presidency, 1982

Elders Vaughn J. Featherstone, Robert L. Backman, Rex D. Pinegar

Baptist ordaining Joseph Smith and Oliver Cowdery to the Aaronic Priesthood was displayed on the uniform, and "AP Scouts" was sewn above the left pocket. With the approval of Elder Hales, training meetings were conducted throughout Church stakes in Germany, and in other stakes and missions throughout Europe, introducing local Church leaders to the Scouting program. A highlight of AP Scouting was an AP Scout Jamboree held in 1989 near Stuttgart, Germany. Over 2,000 European LDS Scouts and leaders from many nations attended. Special emphasis was placed on young men connecting to their fathers and leaders in outdoor settings.

AP Scout neckerchief

Aaronic Priesthood Scouting (AP Scouts) was organized in Europe in 1983 under the direction of Elder Robert L. Backman, Young Men General President; Elder Hans Ringger, Regional Representative from Basel, Switzerland; and Elder Robert D. Hales, Area Authority in Frankfurt, Germany. Brothers Juergen Warnke, Juergen Fischer, and James Backman were called and set apart as the European Area Scouting Committee. When a favorable affiliation could not be established between the Church and local Scouting groups, the brethren were directed to design a Church Scouting program. Scout handbooks from Ireland, England, Canada, Holland, Austria, Switzerland, Germany, Australia, and the United States were used as references. Merit badges included subjects such as genealogy and scripture study as well as traditional Scouting skills. Standard uniforms were ordered from outdoor clothing companies, and special merit badges and insignia were designed and made by the Church Distribution Center. A logo depicting John the

Scouts in Stuttgart, Germany, cook their dinner over an open fire.

200 million service hours were logged in 2000 through the combined efforts of Boy Scout youth and leaders.

CHAPTER 8

A NEW MILLENNIUM OF SCOUTING
2000–2013

"Be Prepared" and "Do a good turn daily" . . . include two of the shortest verbs in the English language, "Be" and "Do". The idea of living and doing is one of tying knots that will hold under pressure. Poorly tied knots are evident in career, business and marriage failures. To be able to tie the right knot for the right reason, for the right occasion, and to have it hold against every stress is a part of the process of being prepared.

—President Gordon B. Hinckley

President Gordon B. Hinckley

The Denali Award was introduced in 2001 for Varsity Scouts.

The opening of the twenty-first century was marked with notable milestones for the Boy Scouts of America and The Church of Jesus Christ of Latter-day Saints. The 100 millionth youth member was registered in the National Organization. Approximately 410,805 of these Scouts were registered in LDS units. Young men faced increasing moral and spiritual challenges in the new century, and renewed emphasis was placed on Aaronic Priesthood and Primary boys accomplishing hard things through outdoor Scouting activities.

Terrorist attacks in New York City on September 11, 2001, sparked service projects and good turns throughout the country. "Good Turn for America" partnered the BSA with organizations such as the Salvation Army, the American Red Cross, and Habitat for Humanity, providing opportunities for Scouting units to address issues of hunger, homelessness, inadequate housing, and poor health through service. LDS Scouts willingly participated in these nationwide good turns and service.

The centennial of the Boy Scout movement was commemorated in 2007. During a special broadcast on May 12, President Thomas S. Monson spoke to Aaronic Priesthood and LDS Scout leaders and emphasized using the Scouting program as a way to build character.

Three Fulfilling our Duty to God *booklets were available in 2001, one for each age group*

Fulfilling Our
Duty
to God

Past Young Men general presidents and presidency members with President Thomas S. Monson in 2009. From left to right: Elder Robert K. Dellenbach, Elder Robert L. Backman, Elder Jack H. Goaslind, Brother Dean R. Burgess, Elder Vaughn J. Featherstone, President Thomas S. Monson, Brother Charles W. Dahlquist II, Elder F. Melvin Hammond, Brother Michael A. Neider

In 1999, an *Aaronic Priesthood Achievement* program was developed for use in areas outside of the United States and Canada. It provided an activity program for young men ages twelve through eighteen and was recommended for use when church affiliations with national Scouting organizations were not possible.

Aaronic Priesthood: Fulfilling our Duty to God, an achievement program with both Scouting and religious requirements, was approved in 2001 for use in the United States and Canada. It replaced the original 1954 *Duty to God* program, and was adapted from the international *Aaronic Priesthood*

Achievement program of 1999. Its purpose was to help young men learn and fulfill priesthood duties. Requirements included Scouting goals and achievements, and young men were encouraged to earn their Eagle Scout award.

In 2010, the Church published *Fulfilling My Duty to God,* a booklet that replaced the previous *Fulfilling Our Duty to God* program. The new booklet was used for all three Aaronic Priesthood quorums and contained more individual goal setting and an emphasis on "Learn, Act, Share." It was intended to be used by LDS youth throughout the world.

"Scouting contributes to a boy's preparation to hold the priesthood of God. Scout leaders have a sacred responsibility. They help boys learn Scouting principles that also help them live the gospel."

—Rosemary M. Wixom, Primary general president, 2010

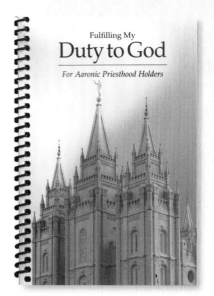

Fulfilling My Duty to God, 2010

"Becoming the Magnificent Priesthood"

Oil painting by Anne Marie Oborn

A Cub Scout with the 2003
Faith in God *booklet*

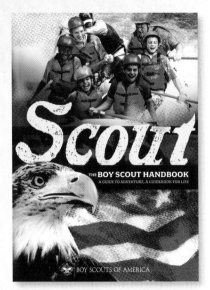

The twelfth edition of the Boy Scout Handbook was issued in 2009, printed on recycled paper. It included elements of previous editions as well as an interactive iPhone app.

One World, One Promise.

Elder F. Melvin Hammond, Young Men general president, 2001-2004, with Scouts at the 2003 World Scout Jamboree in Thailand.

Charles Dahlquist, Young Men general president, 2004-2009, visits with Scouts at the 2007 World Scout Jamboree.

World Scout Jamborees

The Church continues to affiliate wherever possible with international Scouting organizations. Currently, Church Scouting programs are active in Austria, Switzerland, Tahiti, Argentina, Brazil, and other parts of the world.

Church leaders consistently participate in and attend international Scouting events. A world Scout jamboree was held in England in 2007, commemorating the centennial of the Scouting movement. Events included a re-enactment of the camp at Brownsea Island. Over 38,000 Scouts from 158 countries attended. The 2011 World Scout Jamboree held in Rinkaby, Sweden, was a gathering of over 40,000 Scouts representing 143 nations around the world. Over 200 LDS Scouts and leaders were present from the United States, Tahiti, Sweden, Italy, Canada, Uganda, and other countries.

"Young men and their leaders should be as a light to the world. Collectively, you should be like a city on a hill that cannot be hid. Individually and collectively, you should be an example of living the Scout Oath, Law, Motto and Slogan."

—David L. Beck, Young Men general president, *Church News*, July 24, 2010

LDS Scouts sing during the 2011 World Jamboree Lighthouse Service, highlighting major religions of the earth.

David L. Beck, Young Men general president; Europe Area president Elder Erich W. Kopischke of the Seventy; Scouter Gail Roper; Elder Ingvar Olsson of the Seventy; and Larry M. Gibson, first counselor, Young Men general presidency at the 2011 World Jamboree in Rinkaby, Sweden.

International flags welcome visitors to the 2011 World Jamboree.

National Scout Jamborees

Church leaders actively support national Scout jamborees. An LDS exhibit at each jamboree gives visitors a chance to learn about Church standards and principles. In addition, the Genealogy and Family Life merit badges are offered. The 2010 National Jamboree was the final jamboree held at Fort A.P. Hill in Virginia, and commemorated the centennial of the Boy Scouts of America. Charles W. Dahlquist II, former Young Men general president, served as head chaplain of all faiths.

Elder Robert D. Hales visits with Scouts at the 2010 National Jamboree.

President Thomas S. Monson at the 2005 National Jamboree

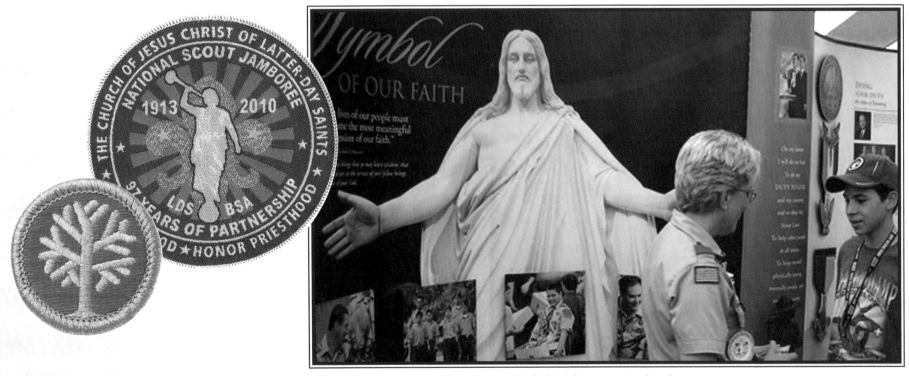

Church Faith and Beliefs exhibit at a national jamboree

Scuba diving offers Scouts an adventure at the 2010 National Jamboree.

LDS Scouts sing at the 2005 National Jamboree.

*LDS Scouts at the 2010 National Jamboree earned
the George Albert Smith Award.*

Aaronic Priesthood Encampments

In various areas of North America, Aaronic Priesthood encampments are held on a stake and multistake basis. The purpose of the encampments is to provide meaningful and challenging activities to prepare young men for future spiritual and physical challenges, and to teach them to accomplish hard things. Gatherings are often held at Boy Scouts of America camps and facilities, utilizing Scouting resources and outdoor programs, as well as the safety provided by the National Organization. Activities are generally based on scriptural people and events, such as King Benjamin, Captain Moroni, and Joseph Smith, and include merit badges, water-front activities, and the various high adventure programs that are available at Scout camps. Resources, activities, and firesides help young men understand and fulfill their priesthood duties, prepare for the blessings of the temple, effectively serve full-time missions, and be worthy husbands and fathers.

Aaronic Priesthood encampments continue to be held throughout the Church, with many planned in conjunction with the LDS-BSA centennial in 2013.

2013 is the 50th anniversary of the Philmont Priesthood Leadership Conferences.

Well-known Scouter and wood carver Bill Burch demonstrates his artistry.

Families call tent city home while at Philmont.

Priesthood Leadership Conferences

The Church's use of the BSA Philmont Training Center to conduct training for priesthood leaders continues to expand. In 2007 the Church funded an extensive remodel of the LDS chapel at Philmont, repairing damage and updating windows, doors and wiring. In addition, yearly priesthood leadership conferences are coordinated by the LDS-BSA Relationships director, and held under the direction of the Young Men general presidency with the Primary general presidency. Stake presidents and family members are invited to attend one of the two week-long courses.

Sister Rosemary Wixom, Primary general president, spends time with Cub Scouts at Philmont.

The Primary parade is a highlight of Philmont family events.

Wayne Perry of Seattle, Washington, was appointed in 2012 to serve as the National BSA President, the first Church member ever to hold this position.

BSA 2012 statistical reports cite the LDS Church as the largest chartered organization of the Boy Scouts of America, sponsoring 37,856 units and 430,557 youth.

"Scouting is fun and has an important purpose! Woven through all the fun is an inspired program that really works.... Scouting prepares boys to become righteous men who hold and honor the priesthood of God."

—Cheryl C. Lant, Primary general president, 2005-2010

The Thomas S. Monson Award was created for the 2013 National Jamboree.

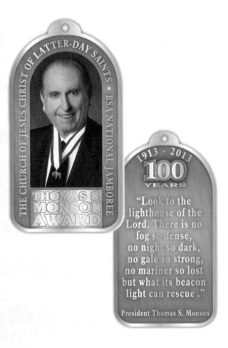

Priesthood holders prepare the sacrament at the 2005 National Jamboree.

One hundred years have passed since the affiliation of The Church of Jesus Christ of Latter-day Saints and the Boy Scouts of America. During the past century, millions of youth and leaders—both members and nonmembers of the Church—have been blessed through LDS Scouting involvement. The Boy Scout Promise to live "On my honor" has remained unchanged during the past century.

Cub Scouts and Eleven-year-old Scouts continue under the direction of the Primary. Their combined membership makes up more than 50 percent of LDS Scouts.

Church leaders, including members of the Young Men and Primary general presidencies, serve on the National Executive Board and advisory committees of the Boy Scouts of America. President Monson retains his active status as the longest-tenured member of the board, serving since 1969.

The 2013 National Jamboree will be the first held at the new Summit Bechtel Reserve in West Virginia. A Monday evening stadium show, produced by the Church, will commemorate their century-old Scouting affiliation and will be viewed by thousands of youth and leaders.

The commemoration of the LDS-BSA centennial includes an exhibit, "A Good Turn Daily: 100 Years of Scouting and the Aaronic Priesthood," at the LDS Church History Museum, and a grand celebration at the Conference Center.

The inspired decision made one hundred years ago to affiliate Scouting programs of The Church of Jesus Christ of Latter-day Saints and the Boy Scouts of America has resulted in countless good turns, strong relationships, and millions of lives positively affected by both organizations. A century later, this Scouting partnership continues to enable young men to successfully serve as missionaries, husbands, and fathers and fulfill their duty to God, country, and family. The legacy of these youth and their dedicated leaders has indeed created a century of honor.

LDS-BSA Centennial
commemorative memorabilia

"A Good Turn Daily: 100 Years of
Scouting and the Aaronic Priesthood"
Church History Museum exhibit
July–December 2013

"Scouting brings out the best in each of us. . . .
May you uphold Scouting's tradition, for it can be as a lighthouse beacon in the world of stormy seas, it can be a motivation to prepare for your role in life, it can be a yardstick against which you measure your accomplishments."
—President Thomas S. Monson

100 YEARS OF SCOUTING IN THE LDS CHURCH

Young Men are organized by Junius F. Wells on June 10—to be called "Young Men's Mutual Improvement Association" (YMMIA).

The *Contributor* magazine becomes the voice of the new YMMIA.

The *Improvement Era* replaces the *Contributor* as the official YMMIA publication.

Colonel Robert Baden-Powell writes *Aids to Scouting* to train his soldiers in outdoor and self-reliant skills.

Baden-Powell rewrites *Aids to Scouting* for boys and tests his theories at a Scout encampment on Brownsea Island, summer 1907.

Scouting for Boys, Part 1 of 6, hits the newsstands in January and is an instant success. Scout units form around the world.

1875   **1876**   **1897**   **1899**   **1907**   **1908**

War Service flourishes as Scouts perform "good turns" such as planting war gardens and selling Liberty Bonds and Thrift Stamps.

Local councils are created in Utah, with the Ogden and Salt Lake Councils in 1919, and Utah County in 1921. The Salt Lake Council's first Scout Executive is Oscar Kirkham.

The BSA is divided into twelve regions. Region 12 includes Utah, Arizona, Nevada, and California.

The Church MIA celebrates 25 years of youth programs. Special editions of the *Improvement Era* are published in June and July.

The Church organizes the Vanguard program for older boys ages 15-16 and gains national BSA approval.

In 1928, the LDS Church names Scouting as the activity program for deacons and teachers (ages 12-16).

1917   **1919**   **1920**   **1925**   **1928**

William D. Boyce incorporates the Boy Scouts of America (BSA) on February 8, the result of a good turn from an unknown English Scout.

The first Utah Scout unit is formed by Thomas George Wood in the Waterloo Ward on October 12, 1910.

MIA Scouts are organized by the LDS Church on November 29, following the format and activities found in Scout books of the day.

The LDS Church joins the Boy Scouts of America on May 21, 1913, as the BSA's first chartered organization, setting the pattern for other organizations to sponsor Scout groups.

John H. Taylor becomes the first LDS Scout Commissioner, serving all LDS units in the western United States.

A Congressional Charter is granted to the Boy Scouts of America on June 15.

1910   1911   1913   1916

The 100th Anniversary of the Church is celebrated with a new song for youth, "Carry On." It becomes the MIA theme song.

Though the BSA made Cubbing official in 1933, Cub Scouts do not become part of the Church's program for another 19 years.

The BSA celebrates its Silver Jubilee (25 years of Scouting) in February. To date, there are 25,000 registered LDS Scouts and Vanguards in 22 countries.

7,000 Vanguards became Explorer Scouts in June, 1935, as they merge with the BSA's new program, which is based on the LDS Vanguard program.

The anniversary of 25 years of Scouting in the Church is celebrated June 10-12 with many events, including a huge Cavalcade of Scouting with 5,000 boys attending.

World War II, 1941-45, brings much hardship but also allows for many good turns. Young men 18 years old are drafted, so Explorer Scouts are now ages 15-17.

1930   1935   1938   1941

Explorer units are called "Posts." A new green uniform and "Ranger" advancement program are introduced.

A Deseret Recognition award is created for LDS Explorer Scouts.

The 100th Anniversary of pioneers entering the Salt Lake Valley is celebrated with a Centennial Campout July 21-25. Four thousand Scouts from the U.S. and Mexico attend.

Scouting entry age changes to 11. All boys 14 and older are now Explorers.

President David O. McKay announces a Church-Scouting Relationships Committee on October 24.

Primary sponsors Cub Scouting, and 11-year-old Scouts change to a Guide Patrol under the direction of the Primary Association.

1944 1945 1947 1949 1951 1952

Webelos Rank replaces Lion in an attempt to hold the interest of older Cub Scout boys.

The Duty to God Trail award program begins a year later.

LaVern Parmley, Primary general president, becomes one of the first women to serve on a national Scout committee. In 1976, she is the first woman to receive the Silver Buffalo award.

The BSA's Career-Emphasis Exploring Program now includes girls.
Venturing is created in the Church to meet the needs of young men ages 14-15.

Blazer Patrol replaces Guide Patrol (11-year-old Scouts) in the Primary in 1970.
In 1971, the *New Era* replaces the *Improvement Era*.

The MIA is placed under the direction of the Presiding Bishopric. Then, in 1977 the name is changed to Young Men, and a Young Men Presidency is reinstated.

An On My Honor award is introduced for LDS Scouts ages 12-18, and Duty to God Scouting requirements are removed.

1967 1969 1970 1974 1977

The Duty to God award is created for boys 12-18, correlating Scouting and priesthood responsibilities.

A new Vanguard Program provides Scouting for LDS boys 12-14 outside of the U.S. (different from the 1928 Scout program for older boys).

Exploring replaces the old Explorer program with a new logo and exciting activities.

The BSA celebrates 50 years of Scouting in the U.S. with a Golden Jubilee.

A 50 Golden Years of Scouting in the Church celebration is held February 1.

First Philmont Priesthood Leadership Conference held June 5-11.

The Church makes a "Recommittal to Scouting" during a special broadcast. A Canada-U.S. encampment is held in Farragut, Idaho, in July, and 3500 boys attend.

Guide Patrol Day Camps begin under the direction of the Primary.

1954   1957   1959   1960   1963   1966

Varsity Scouting is developed by LDS leaders in Utah. The 1978 pilot program replaces the Church's Venturing program (boys age 14-15) in 1983 and becomes a National BSA program in 1984.

The Faith in God award, announced in 1978, recognizes Cub Scout boys in Primary.

The Church's Consolidated Meeting Schedule combines religious instruction on Sunday, allowing more time during Mutual for Scouting activities.

The Duty to God Trail award program ends in 1982.

The BSA Diamond Jubilee (75 years of Scouting) is celebrated with a special Church broadcast and a unique patch.

The Explorer Leadership Conference (E^2) for priest-age boys, 16-18, is directed by the Young Men general presidency at Philmont.

1978   1980   1982   1985

The 75th anniversary of Scouting in The Church of Jesus Christ of Latter-day Saints is celebrated with a special Baden-Powell patch and a commemorative broadcast.

A New Scout patrol is created by the National BSA based on the Church's Scout program for 11-year-olds. Blazer Scouts are renamed Eleven-year-old Scouts in 1995.

Budget allowance changes include many Scouting costs. The Church now pays for activities and registration, excluding long-term camps.

A new BSA Venturing Program replaces the Exploring program, February 9. It resembles the 1928 Vanguard and 1940s-50s Exploring programs, with outdoor emphasis and Ranger and Silver awards.

1988   1990   1991   1998

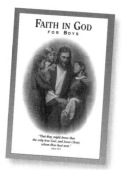

The Duty to God Aaronic Priesthood program contains both Scouting and priesthood requirements. Separate books are used for each quorum, and boys earn a medallion. Primary replaces the Faith in God award with new requirements and no medal.

100 years of Scouting is celebrated with a World Jamboree in England. A unique patch in many languages shares the theme, "One World, One Promise."

BSA celebrates 100 Years of Scouting with a year-long series of activities and a National Jamboree, the last one held at Fort A.P. Hill in Virginia. The Church creates a patch and George Albert Smith Award.

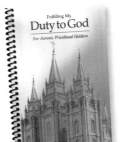

Fulfilling My Duty to God replaces the 2001 program. One book is used for all quorums, with more individual goal setting and a "Learn, Act, Share" emphasis.

100 Years of Scouting in the LDS Church is celebrated with an exhibit at the Church History Museum July–December and a grand commemoration in October.

2001   2007   2010   2013

LDS SCOUTING GROWTH THROUGH THE YEARS

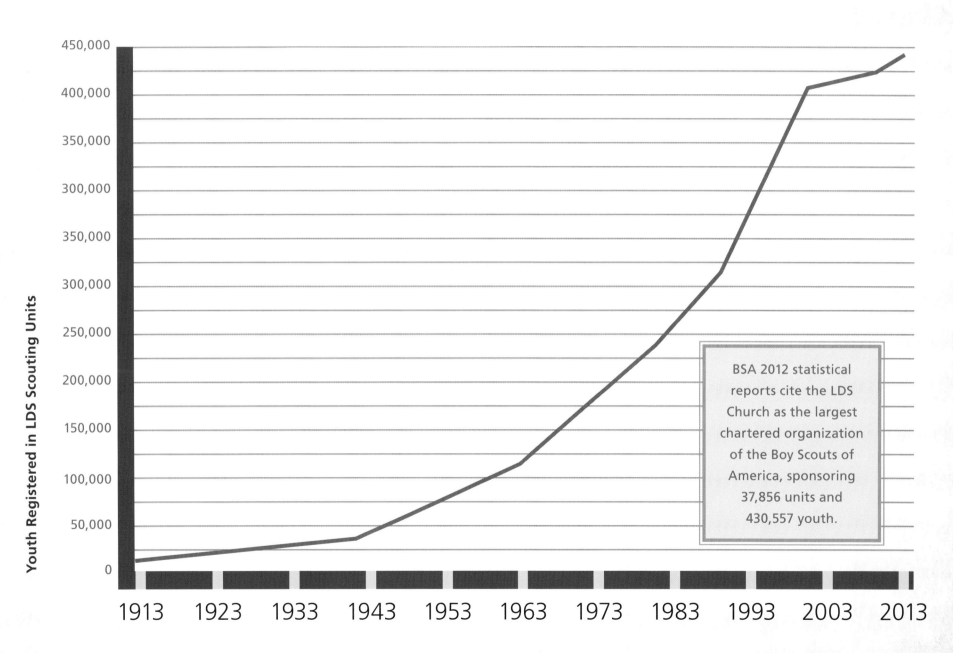

Youth Registered in LDS Scouting Units

450,000
400,000
350,000
300,000
350,000
300,000
250,000
200,000
150,000
100,000
50,000
0

BSA 2012 statistical reports cite the LDS Church as the largest chartered organization of the Boy Scouts of America, sponsoring 37,856 units and 430,557 youth.

1913   1923   1933   1943   1953   1963   1973   1983   1993   2003   2013

YOUNG MEN AND PRIMARY GENERAL PRESIDENTS

Young Men General Presidents

1876–1880
Junius F. Wells

1880–1898
Wilford Woodruff

1898–1901
Lorenzo Snow

1901–1918
Joseph F. Smith

1918–1921
Anthony W. Ivins

1921–1935
George Albert Smith

1935–1937
Albert E. Bowen

1937–1948
George Q. Morris

1948–1958
Elbert R. Curtis

1958–1962
Joseph T. Bentley

1962–1969
G. Carlos Smith Jr.

1969–1972
W. Jay Eldredge

1972–1974
Robert L. Backman

1974–1977
Victor L. Brown

1977–1979
Neil D. Schaerrer

1979–1985
Robert L. Backman

1985–1990
Vaughn J. Featherstone

1990–1998
Jack H. Goaslind

1998–2001
Robert K. Dellenbach

2001–2004
F. Melvin Hammond

2004–2009
Charles W. Dahlquist II

2009–
David L. Beck

Note: Leaders of the Young Men's Mutual Improvement Association were referred to as superintendents. In 1974, Presiding Bishop Victor L. Brown was given jurisdiction over the young men. In 1977, the Young Men organization was restructured, and a presidency was called. All presidents since then have been members of the First Quorum of the Seventy, except Neil D. Schaerrer, Charles W. Dahlquist II, and David L. Beck.

Primary General Presidents

 1880–1925
Louie B. Felt

 1925–1939
May Anderson

 1940–1943
May Green Hinckley

 1943–1951
Adele C. Howells

 1951–1974
LaVern W. Parmley

 1974–1980
Naomi M. Shumway

 1980–1988
Dwan J. Young

 1988–1994
Michaelene P. Grassli

 1994–1999
Patricia P. Pinegar

 1999–2005
Coleen K. Menlove

 2005–2010
Cheryl C. Lant

 2010–
Rosemary M. Wixom

LDS-BSA RELATIONSHIPS DIRECTORS

The position of Church Scout Commissioner originated with the organization of the MIA Scouts in 1911, and continued after affiliation with the Boy Scouts of America in 1913. The appointed individual was called by Church authorities and was responsible to oversee Scouting activities within the Church and work as a liaison between the two organizations. In 1951, at the request of Elder Ezra Taft Benson, the responsibility became a full-time paid professional position of the Boy Scouts of America. The Director of Mormon Relationships (later changed to LDS-BSA Relationships) was appointed by mutual agreement between the Church and national Scouting leaders. The appointed individual was required to be a priesthood bearer.

1913
John H. Taylor

1919
Oscar A. Kirkham

1947
Rock M. Kirkham

1950–1964
D. L. "Lou" Roberts

1964–1974
Folkman D. Brown

1974–ca. 1980
Ross J. Taylor

ca. 1980–1988
John Warnick

1988–1992
Robert M. Mills

1992–2001
K. Hart Bullock

2001–2006
C. Bradford Allen

2007–2012
David C. Pack

2012
C. Bradford Allen

2013–
Mark R. Francis

PROMINENT SCOUTING AWARD RECIPIENTS

Bronze Wolf

Ezra Taft Benson

Thomas S. Monson

Silver World Award

Spencer W. Kimball

Silver Buffalo

Robert L. Backman

Ezra Taft Benson

Elbert R. Curtis

Charles W. Dahlquist II

Vaughn J. Featherstone

Jack H. Goaslind

Heber J. Grant

F. Melvin Hammond

Marion D. Hanks

George R. Hill III

Gordon B. Hinckley

Spencer W. Kimball

Harold B. Lee

David O. McKay

Coleen K. Menlove

Thomas S. Monson

LaVern W. Parmley

George Albert Smith

Delbert L. Stapley

N. Eldon Tanner

Lance B. Wickman

Dwan Jacobsen Young

Silver Antelope

Marvin J. Ashton

Robert L. Backman

David L. Beck

Ezra Taft Benson

Dean R. Burgess

Elbert R. Curtis

Charles W. Dahlquist II

Robert K. Dellenbach

Vaughn J. Featherstone

Larry M. Gibson

Michaelene P. Grassli

Marion D. Hanks

George R. Hill III

Oscar A. Kirkham

Cheryl Lant

David O. McKay

George Q. Morris

Michael A. Neider

LaVern W. Parmley

Mark E. Petersen

Rex D. Pinegar

Sydney Reynolds

LeGrand Richards

Naomi Shumway

Robert L. Simpson

G. Carlos Smith Jr.

Delbert L. Stapley

Dwan Jacobsen Young

Distinguished Eagle Scout

Marvin J. Ashton

Robert L. Backman

Vaughn J. Featherstone

Larry M. Gibson

John H. Groberg

Jeffrey R. Holland

Howard W. Hunter

Dallin H. Oaks

H. Burke Peterson

Steven E. Snow

CHURCH MAGAZINE SCOUTING COVERS

Juvenile Instructor

February 1919

Juvenile Instructor

July 1920

Improvement Era

March 1929

Improvement Era

August 1936

Improvement Era

June 1938

Improvement Era

April 1960

Improvement Era

July 1960

Improvement Era

February 1963

Improvement Era

February 1967

New Era

May 1974

New Era

May 1984

New Era

October 1984

New Era

June 1986

Children's Friend

September 1945

Improvement Era

February 1950

Improvement Era

February 1951

Improvement Era

July 1952

Improvement Era

June 1953

New Era

June 1974

New Era

October 1980

New Era

December 1980

New Era

May 1981

New Era

May 1983

New Era

May 2001

New Era

April 2007

New Era

February 2010

ACKNOWLEDGMENTS

Century of Honor: 100 Years of Scouting in The Church of Jesus Christ of Latter-day Saints was compiled at the request of the Young Men General Presidency: David L. Beck, Young Men General President; Larry M. Gibson, First Counselor; and Adrian Ochoa, Second Counselor, and under the direction of Mark R. Francis, LDS-BSA Relationships Director. Former and current Young Men and Primary general presidency members also provided input. The text, photographs, and artifacts were compiled through the cooperative efforts of several individuals and institutions. Their tremendous work and tireless dedication contributed to the production of this timely publication.

LDS–BSA Centennial Book Committee

Christine Cox, Manager, Public Services, Church History Library

Nettie H. Francis, Project Manager, Writer

Kevin V. Hunt, Scouting Historian

Corry Kanzenberg, Curator, National Scouting Museum

Stacie Lusk, Intern, Church History Museum

Dale R. McClellan, Administrative Assistant, Priesthood Department

Steven Price, Archivist, National Scouting Museum

Kathi Robertson, Scouting Historian

Alex Stromberg, Intern, Church History Museum

Additional gratitude is expressed for the talents and assistance of the following:

John Gibby, Art Director

Shauna Gibby, Designer

Stephen Hall, Administrative Assistant, Young Men General Presidency

Daniel Hogan, Copy Editor

Heidi H. Meservy, Research Assistant

Joanne Reinertson, Administrative Assistant, LDS-BSA Relationships Office

Members of the 1913 Society

NOTES

page v   Thomas S. Monson, *Ensign,* Nov. 1993.

Chapter 1

Epigraph: *Improvement Era,* Mar. 1912, 359.

1. Davis Bitton, "Zion's Rowdies: Growing up on the Mormon Frontier," *Utah Historical Quarterly* 50 (Spring 1982), 182-95; as quoted in *Men to Boys,* 51.

2. Junius F. Wells, "Historical Sketch of the YMMIA," *Improvement Era,* June 1925, 714.

3. Ibid, 714-16.

4. http://en.wikipedia.org/wiki/Young_Men_(organization) (March 6, 2013).

5. First Presidency Circular, July 11, 1877, 4.

6. Edward L. Rowan, *To Do My Best: James E. West and the History of the Boy Scouts of America* (2007), 30.

7. *Improvement Era,* May 1903, 545.

8. Joseph F. Smith, "Opening Address," Seventy-eighth Annual Conference of The Church of Jesus Christ of Latter-day Saints, 1908, 6.

9. *Improvement Era,* Jan. 1909, 247.

10. Letter from Bryant S. Hinckley to "Friend" (undated), Deseret Gym Records, 10.

Chapter 2

Epigraph: Address to Scout/Guide Commisioners' Conference, 2 July 1926.

11. Thomas George Wood Diary, vol. 13, Sep. 5–Oct. 3, 1910.

12. Thomas George Wood Writings, 21.

Chapter 3

Epigraph: *Improvement Era,* Oct. 1911, 1089-90.

13. *Improvement Era,* Apr. 1911, 539-43.

14. *Improvement Era,* Apr. 1911, 539-43.

15. *Improvement Era,* Feb. 1963, 90-91.

Chapter 4

Epigraph: *Headquarters Gazette,* Nov. 1920.

16. *Improvement Era,* Sep. 1913, 1135.

17. *Improvement Era,* Apr. 1960, 272.

18. Letter to the General Superintendent and General Board of YMMIA, February 19, 1913.

19. Letter to John H. Taylor from James E. West, January 29, 1913.

20. *Fourth Annual Report of the Boy Scouts of America,* Feb. 12, 1914, 20.

21. *Improvement Era,* Feb. 1918, 366-74.

22. Federal Charter, Article XI, Section 3, Boy Scout Constitution.

Chapter 5

Epigraph: *Improvement Era,* Feb. 1935, 77-78.

23. *Improvement Era,* Apr. 1921, 467.

24. Carol Cornwall Madsen and Susan Staker Oman, *Sisters and Little Saints,* Deseret Book Company, 1979, 82–83.

25. *Improvement Era,* Apr. 1930, 389.

Chapter 6

Epigraph: *Improvement Era,* Sep. 1948, 558.

26. Robert Ellis, "Getting the Message Out: The Poster Boys of World War II, Part 2," National Archives, *Prologue Magazine,* Summer 2005, vol. 37, no. 2.

27. YMMIA General Board Minutes, Jan. 1942, 47.

28. *Boys' Life,* Feb. 1946, 3.

29. *Improvement Era,* Jan. 1947, 21.

30. *Improvement Era,* Jun. 1953, 470.

31. First Presidency Circular, Dec. 31, 1952.

32. Carol Cornwall Madsen and Susan Staker Oman, *Sisters and Little Saints,* Deseret Book Company, 1979, 137–38, 141.

33. First Presidency Circular, Feb. 5, 1965.

34. *Aaronic Priesthood Youth Including YMMIA,* 1970, 5.

Chapter 7

Epigraph: *Ensign,* May 1977.

35. *Church News,* Jun. 23, 1973.

36. First Presidency Circular, May 22, 1973.

37. *Ensign,* Jan. 1984, 79–80.

38. http://www.merriam-webster.com/dictionary/jamboree.

39. First Presidency Circular, October 26, 1988.

Chapter 8

Epigraph: *Church News,* Feb. 10, 1985, 3, 11.

Page 99: www.lds.org/callings/primary/leader-resources/scouting-in-primary?lang=eng

Page 109: "Strengths of Scouting" video, lds.org, 2010.

Back Cover

Thomas S. Monson, "Welcome Rain," Las Vegas Scout Encampment, Oct. 14, 2006.

LIST OF VISUALS

Courtesy Boy Scouts of America: ix, Mark Francis; 8, Brownsea Island; 9, Baden-Powell military attire; 10, Baden Powell Scout Uniform; 11, William D. Boyce; 12, James E. West; 13, Helping Lady; 34, 1911 fleur-de-lis; 39, Congressional Charter; 42, War garden; 43, Selling Liberty bonds; 43, Collecting peach pits; 45, 1920 World Jamboree; 50, Boys setting up tent; 51, Boys cooking; 60, 1935, 1937 Jamboree patches; 71, D. Lou Roberts; 80, Philmont Scout Ranch Villa; 81, Tooth of Time rock at Philmont Scout Ranch; 86, Explorer Scouts around campfire; 88, Boys hiking across bridge; 91, 1977 National Jamboree; 91, 1973 National Scout Jamboree patch; 94, Scouting for food; 100, *Boy Scout Handbook*, 2009; 101, 2011 World Jamboree flags; 102, Genealogy Merit Badge; 106, Philmont Logo; 107, Wayne Perry; 108, 2013 National Jamboree patch

Courtesy Christine Cox: 2, Boys playing marbles; 4, Boys in Sunday dress; 48, Box Elder News clip, 1925; 49, BSA Troop 5, Brigham City, Utah

Courtesy Church History Library and The Church of Jesus Christ of Latter-day Saints: Cover, Scout band on Temple Square, 1925; ix, Young Men General Presidency, 2009; x, MIA Scout Band; 2, Junius F. Wells; 3, Early *Contributor;* 7, Deseret Gym, circa 1910; 17, First Aetna Scout Troop; 21, John H Taylor; 22, March 1912 *Improvement Era;* 23, June 1912 *Improvement Era,* p. 753; 25, MIA Scouts on the pioneer trail; 25, Jan. 1913 *Improvement Era;* 27, March 1912 *Improvement Era;* 28, Early Scout flag ceremony; 31, Western Scout Shoes ad, March 1913 *Improvement Era;* 32, Official YMMIA Boy Scout Charter; 37, 1913 Athletic Committee; 40, Young Ezra Taft Benson; 40, Aug. 1916 *Improvement Era;* 44, Oscar Kirkham; 46, Scout band on Temple Square, 1925; 48, MIA Boy Scout band in front of Church Administration Building; 49, Brigham H. Roberts; 51, Gordon B Hinckley; 52, George Wharton James with Boy Scouts; 53, Boy Scouts on top of natural bridge; 54, Primary boys prepare for Scouting; 55,

President Howard W. Hunter as a Scout; 56, Emery County Boy Scouts at celebration 1925; 56, *Log of the Vanguard Trail* manual; 58, Scouts at Independence Rock, 1930; 59, Church leaders at Independence Rock, 1930; 60, Boy Scouts at the Hill Cumorah; 61, Boy Scouts at Palmyra, New York; 61, Boy Scouts on the Pony Express Trail; 61, Boy Scouts at Winter Quarters; 62, 1929 Church leaders in Germany, Mar. 1929 *Improvement Era,* p. 436; 62, George Albert Smith with international Scouts; 64, 1938 parade on Main Street; 64, Beneficial Life Scouting ad, back cover of *Improvement Era,* June 1954; 65, June 1938 *Improvement Era* cover; 66, Sept. 1945 *Friend* cover, June 1953 *Improvement Era* cover; 66, Beneficial Life Scouting ad Verso of *Improvement Era,* June 1954; 67, George Albert Smith; 68, Boy Scouts unveil *This Is the Place* monument; 70, President Benson and two Scout sons, 1950s; 70, *George Albert Smith* oil painting by Keith Larson; 71, Church Scouting leaders; 72, Elder Mark E. Petersen with eleven-year-old Scouts; 73, President David O. McKay and Elder Ezra Taft Benson welcome an eleven-year-old boy into Scouting; 74, LaVern Parmley; 75, *Cub Scouting in the Church* manual; 76, Sister Parmley with Scouts at Colorado Springs jamboree, 1960; 77, *Exploring into Manhood;* 78, David O. McKay with Scouts; 82, Scouts around a radio; 83, Feb. 1967 *Improvement Era* cover; 83, *Coeur d'Alene Press* for Saturday, July 30, 1966; 87, President Kimball and Explorer Scout; 87, three Church Scouting medals; 89, *New Era* magazine covers; 90, President Ezra Taft Benson, Salt Lake Tabernacle, 1985; 95, 1982 Young Men General Presidency; 99, 2010 *Duty to God* booklet; 99, Cub Scout with *Faith in God* booklet; 102, Faith and Beliefs exhibit, 2005 National Jamboree; 120-121, Church Magazine Covers

Courtesy Church History Museum: 47, Boy Scout band banner; 54, Trail Builder Log, Bandlo, Cap; 95, AP Scouts neckerchief; 109, "Camp Good Turn: 100 Years of Scouting in the Church" logo

Courtesy Dale McClellan: 63, Eagle Scouts in Colonia Juarez, Mexico; 66, Colonia Juarez, Mexico Scout charter; 81, LDS Conference faculty members, 1965; 93, Philmont chapel; 107, Philmont parade; 107, Sister Wixom and Cub Scouts

Courtesy *Deseret News* (Jeffrey D. Allred): 103, Scouts sing at 2005 National Jamboree; 108, Scouts bless the sacrament at the 2010 National Jamboree

Courtesy Great Salt Lake Council: 3, Boys cleaning church; 16, Waterloo Ward Scout Troop in Parley's Canyon; 16, Boys in Trolley Car; 18, Group of boys ready to camp; 20, Two boys with pelts and basket pack; 23, Three boys in outdoors; 24, Boys and puppy dogs; 36, Early Scoutmasters; 96, Boy Scouts on a service mission

© by Intellectual Reserve, Inc.: xi, May 3rd, 1913 letter from James E. West; 6, Bryant S. Hinckley; 19, *Joseph F. Smith* by John Willard Clawson; 29, Lyman Martineau; 35, 1913 Athletic Committee signatures, Affiliation resolution; 45, Heber J. Grant at 1937 World Jamboree; 47, *Heber J. Grant* by C.J. Fox; 57, Ruth May Fox; 62, Boy Scout group in Nuku'alofa, Tonga; 76, Belle S. Spafford; 83, Elder Thomas S. Monson; 83, *For the Strength of Youth,* 1965 pamphlet; 85, Spencer W. Kimball; 90, President Ezra Taft Benson, 1977 National Jamboree; 94, Michaelene P. Grassli; 97, Gordon B Hinckley; 98, 2001 *Duty to God* booklets; 116 – 117, Young Men and Primary General Presidents

Courtesy *Church News,* (Jason Swenson): 98, Former Young Men Presidents meet with President Monson; 102, Elder Robert D. Hales at 2010 National Jamboree; 102, President Monson at 2005 National Jamboree; 103, Scouts scuba-diving at 2010 National Jamboree; 106, Bill Burch Hands; 106, Philmont Tent City; 106, Philmont Flag Ceremony

Courtesy Kathi Robertson: 9, Aids to Scouting; 10, 26, Scouting for Boys pt V; 17, World Scout Fleur-de-lis pin 1920; 20, *Boys' Life* magazine cover, Mar. 1911; 26, Boy Scouts of

America Official Handbook, 1910; 27, Boy Scouts of America Handbook for Boys, 1911; 33, Wandamere Park postcard; 37, 1913 Scout uniform; 38, Scout helping little girl; 52, Scouts at Bryce Canyon; 55, Cub Scout; 57, Explorer Scout; 65, Cavalcade of Scouting program; 73, Guide Patrol Scarf; 73, Guide Patrol Day Camp Patch; 75, Den Mother and Cub Scout; 75, Cub Scout patches; 77, Duty to God Award 1954; 77, Duty to God Trail Pin; 77, Silver Explorer Award patch; 81, Mormon Conference patch; 81, Philmont Training Center Patch; 82, 1963 International Explorer Conference patch; 83, 1966 LDS Scout Encampment patch; 84, Cub Scout on a monkey bridge; 86, three Explorers; 86, Explorer E patch; 88, Varsity Scout patch and handbook; 90, 1977 National Jamboree Patch; 97, Denali Award; 100, World Scout jamboree patches; 131-132, LDS encampment patches

Courtesy LDS-BSA Relationships Office: ix, LDS-BSA Centennial patch; 94, 1988 Diamond Jubilee patch; 102, LDS-BSA 2010 Jamboree patch; 103, George Albert Smith Award medallion; 106, 50 Years at Philmont patch; 108, Thomas S. Monson award; 109, LDS-BSA centennial coin and pin

Courtesy Mark Francis: 93, Peter Fillerup's statue *Scouting, Road to Manhood;* 105, LDS Encampment Nevada Patch; 131-132, LDS encampment patches

Permission Boy Scouts of America: iv, Norman Rockwell, *I Will Do My Best,* © Brown and Bigelow, Inc.; viii, Norman Rockwell, *We Thank Thee, O' Lord,* © Brown and Bigelow, Inc.; 10, Norman Rockwell, *A Daily Good Turn;* 41, Norman Rockwell, *A Scout is Reverent,* © Brown and Bigelow, Inc.

vii, Priesthood/Scouting boys, Courtesy Deseret Book Company

xii, *The Desires of My Heart,* ©Walter Rane, used by permission

1, *Brother Joseph,* © David Lindsley, used by permission

12, Scouting Founders, Photo courtesy Library of Congress Prints and Photographs Division, Call No. LC-B2- 1270-7

15, Waterloo Ward Scout Troop, courtesy Richard Best Family

15, Thomas George Wood, courtesy Wood Family

19, Joseph F. Smith, John Willard Clawson, © IRI

30, Samuel Moffat, Public Domain

47, Heber J. Grant, C.J. Fox, © IRI

50, Camp Kiesel, courtesy Trapper Trails Council

58-59, 1930 Independence Rock encampment, courtesy Fort Caspar Museum, Casper, Wyoming

61, 1935 National Jamboree card, courtesy Wayne Bishop

67, Scoutmaster membership card, courtesy Wayne Bishop

68, S. Dilworth Young, courtesy Pratt Family Organization

69, Deseret Recognition Award, courtesy Carey Beckstead

82, Elders Allen and Hunsaker with LDS Scouts, courtesy Thomas Hunsaker

92, 1985 Scouting Celebration in Tabernacle, courtesy *Church News*

94, Boys hiking narrows, courtesy Steve Evans

95, LDS Scouts at Stuttgart, Germany encampment, courtesy Thomas Hunsaker

99, *Becoming the Magnificent Priesthood,* © Anne Marie Oborn, used by permission

100, Charles Dahlquist with Scouts at 2007 World Scout Jamboree, courtesy Charles W. Dahlquist II

100, Elder Hammond with Thai Scouts, courtesy Joel Wiest

101, LDS Scouts at 2011 World Jamboree, courtesy Steve Reich

101, Church authorities at 2011 World Jamboree, courtesy Wayne Bishop

104,105, LDS Encampment in Spokane, Washington, © Lon Gibby Media

110-114, LDS Scouting Timeline: courtesy Kathi Robertson

118, LDS-BSA Relationships Directors: J. Taylor, O. Kirkham, Roberts, Brown, courtesy Church History Library; R. Kirkham courtesy Sorensen family; R. Taylor courtesy Great Salt Lake Council; Mills courtesy Robert M. Mills. All other images courtesy Boy Scouts of America.

Boys Scouts of America ®, BSA ®, Be Prepared ®, Boy Scouts ®, Boys' Life ®, Cub Scouts ®, Eagle Scout ®, Jamboree ®, Philmont ®, Scouting ®, Scoutmaster ®, Varsity Scout ®, Venturing ®, logos, uniforms, uniform insignia, are either registered trademarks or trademarks of the Boy Scouts of America in the United States and/or other countries.

INDEX

L. D. S.

SILVER JUBILEE

1938

PIONEER CENTENNIAL SCOUT CAMP
18 47

1963

DUTY TO GOD

PIONEER CAMPOREE

CANADIAN-US-LDS BOY SCOUT ENCAMPMENT
1966

FARRAGUT IDAHO

NORFOLK STAKE CAMPOREE

19 68

JESUS CHRIST OF LATTER DAY SAINTS

CHURCH OF

BOY SCOUT-PRIESTHOOD

1970 "MORMON" ENCAMPMENT

CANADIAN-U.S.

"MORMON" ENCAMPMENT

LETCHWORTH-CUMORAH

1846 1848

U.S. MORMON BATTALION TRAIL

NORFOLK STAKE CAMPOREE

LDS 1972

PIPSICO SCOUT RESERVATION

LDS REGIONAL

19 75

CAMPOREE

MORMON HERITAGE TRAILS

19 82

B.S.A. ENCAMPMENT

HIGH ON THE MOUNTAIN TOP

1982 LDS Jamboree

MORMON ENCAMPMENT

TRUE to the FAITH

NAUVOO 1983

LDS ENCAMPMENT 1984
Cumorah — Letchworth
Thy Paths Our Chosen Way

NORTHWEST AREA L.D.S. SCOUT
19 84
ENCAMPMENT

MORMON SCOUTS
DIAMOND JUBILEE
NATIONAL SCOUT JAMBOREE

CAMP STRAKE-CONROE, TEXAS
1913 – 1988
ZION'S
LDS   BSA
JUBILEE
CAMPOREE

LDS SPRING CAMPOUT
1991

ENSIGNS TO THE NATIONS
LDS BSA
SPFLD, MO. REGION ENCAMPMENT
1993 A.P.

TACOMA REGION L.D.S.
19 93
ENCAMPMENT

MORMON TRAIL SCOUT ENCAMPMENT
1848   1998
A HERITAGE OF SERVICE

LDS CAMPOREE GARLAND
PRESSING FORWARD
2001

THE CHURCH OF JESUS CHRIST OF LATTER-DAY SAINTS
WORLD SCOUT JAMBOREE
20   11
RINKABY, SWEDEN
DUTY TO GOD · HONOR PRIESTHOOD

NORTH FLORIDA COUNCIL
CAMPS SHANDS
CS
DOCTRINE AND COVENANTS 115:5, ARISE AND SHINE FORTH
GATEWAY TO EAGLE
2012

THE CHURCH OF JESUS CHRIST OF LATTER-DAY SAINTS
CELEBRATING 100 YEARS OF SCOUTING
CAMP NAISH · MARCH 2013
DUTY TO GOD & SCOUTING